A Path To Wholeness

D1598270

A PATH TO WHOLENESS
A Lenten Companion

Russell J. Levenson Jr.

CHURCH
PUBLISHING
INCORPORATED

A version of this book was previously published as *Provoking Thoughts* by Insight Press.

Church Publishing
19 East 34th Street
New York, NY 10016
www.churchpublishing.org

Cover artwork by Russell J. Levenson Jr.: *Sun Rising*, oil on canvas.
Cover design by Jennifer Kopec, 2Pug Design
Typeset by Denise Hoff

A record of this book is available from the Library of Congress.

ISBN-13: 978-1-64065-317-7 (paperback)
ISBN-13: 978-1-64065-318-4 (ebook)

With gratitude
A Path to Wholeness
Is dedicated to
My mentors
My wife
My children and grandchildren
But above all to
My Lord and Savior Jesus
Who does, and will,
Make whole the lives of
His sheep

Contents

Preface: Before We Begin . . .

"Follow me . . ."

—Matthew 4:19

Augustine wrote that his heart was restless until it found its rest in God. C.S. Lewis once spoke of the human heart as having a "God-shaped hole" that remained incomplete until God filled it. Lord George Carey wrote, "We are living in a fragmented society whose most serious dislocation is between the human and the divine."[1]

The ache of the human heart has always been to be made whole. The thrust of the Christian hope is that we come to that wholeness in a personal relationship with God, through Christ. This book is intentionally written to open one more avenue toward deepening, strengthening, and—for some—maybe birthing such a relationship. It is crafted as a Lenten companion, beginning with Ash Wednesday and carrying us through Easter Day with one additional meditation—but one does not have to limit its use to Lent. All of us need times of reflection and renewal, and they are not necessarily synced to a particular season or time of the year.

A few caveats before we begin. Obviously, as with any writer's work, I offer an understanding of God and God's redemptive work in Christ through my own lens. That lens is molded by a firm commitment to the authority of Holy Scripture; the traditions of the church; dozens of mentors, teachers, and writers; and finally, through my years of service as an ordained priest. I write from the perspective of one who believes in the central truths of Christianity, so it will be clear that some things are assumed in my writing, particularly that the reader will either have an ongoing relationship with God or is, at the very least, interested in having one.

---

1   George Carey, *I Believe* (Harrisburg, PA: Morehouse, 1991), 20.

The reader will also find that I make use of the wisdom of others and of stories to help build each meditation. I also write from a tradition that has historically referred to the Divine predominantly in masculine metaphors, rather than feminine or neuter. When Jesus referred to God, it was primarily as our "heavenly Father"; out of my own reverence, I tend to follow his lead. I do not necessarily believe that God is simply a "great, big man" in the heavens; at times, I refer to God using feminine and androgynous metaphors.

Lastly, let me offer a few words about the structure of the book. Each meditation is introduced by a title, a scripture I have selected, the meditation itself, an occasional photograph, "Another Step . . . ," which is a question to consider in light of the meditation, and a prayer either from the church's tradition or my own hand.

Living in Texas, I have many opportunities to use shotguns. When I was a teenager, I was somewhat of a marksman. The difference between a shotgun and a rifle is the shotgun gives you a greater chance of hitting the target because of the widespread of buckshot. The rifle aims one bullet at the bull's-eye.

I have taken a shotgun approach. I am assuming my readers will come from different places. Some of these meditations may appeal and some may not; some will apply and others will not. While there may be sections of meditations that seem to fit together, for the most part they do not build on each other. Take each meditation as it is intended and prepared: with the hope that some aspect of it will help in making the connection between your need and the provision of God in Christ.

I like the words Jesus used to inaugurate His relationship with each disciple, "Follow me." Not a command. An invitation. They did not have to follow, but they were lovingly invited to do so. It is my profound hope that some piece of this work will invite you to follow as well.

A Prayer

Almighty God,
By Whose spoken Word,
All things came into being;
Speak to us now,
That we may be inspired by your Holy Spirit,
And drawn to follow and proclaim
Jesus Christ as our Lord and our Savior.

—RJL+[2]

---

2 RJL+ denotes a prayer written by Russell J. Levenson Jr.

Seeing Death

Remember how short my time is—for what vanity
you have created all mortals! Who can live and never
see death? Who can escape the power of Sheol?

—Psalm 89:47–48

In the mid-1600s, the "Black Death" or "Black Plague" wiped
out nearly one-third of the population of Europe and the British
Isles. What once felt like ancient history has found new light as
the world has grappled with COVID-19. The cause of the Plague
was a source of great speculation. One theory was it came from
the thick blankets of soot and ash that filled the London skyline.
People began to carry flower petals in their pockets thinking that
might ward off the disease. Groups of victims who were still able
to stand were taken to outside treatment centers. While holding
hands, they would walk in circles around rose gardens, breathing
in the freshness of the blooming flowers and singing what we all
learned as a nursery rhyme:

> Ring around the rosie,
> A pocket full of posies.
> Ashes, ashes, we all fall down.

But they were wrong; people continued to "fall down" until the
real cause of the sickness was determined: flea bites from diseased
rats.

Death is a hard thing to ponder, but it is a good thing to ponder.
It is not unique to our age that people try to postpone or avoid
death. Charlatans were selling life-lengthening tonic water almost
as soon as bottles could be crafted. Hernando De Soto was not the

first to seek the mythical "fountain of youth." Today, all we have to do is turn on late-night television to find pills, herbs, formulas, weight-loss programs, and exercise machines that claim to take the years away. Plastic surgery in the Western world has grown into a veritable industry. Thinking that any of these offers or procedures will protect us from death is no different from placing posies in our pockets. The truth is we all fall down.

"Remember you are dust and to dust you shall return"—these are the most familiar words spoken during the Ash Wednesday services in several Christian traditions.[1] It would be quite depressing if that were all there was to the message, but the gift of death is a reminder of the gift of life itself, of the need to make the most of life while we live it, of the need to live life as it should be lived.

We are all "terminally ill." None of us can escape the power of what the Psalmist calls *Sheol*—the grave. If we know there is a finish line toward which we are all running whether we like it or not, then should it not drive us to make the very most and best of our lives? By "most," I mean should we not learn to feed ourselves with those things that will bless us in every way—physically,

---

1   Genesis 2:7.

emotionally, mentally, spiritually? By "best," should we not seek to live moral, ethical lives? Lives of peace and harmony with God, with our neighbor, with ourselves?

Many see death as an enemy to be avoided. Perhaps it can be a companion along life's journey to remind us to make the most and the best of it.

—— *Another Step . . .* ——
If there was one phrase by which you would like to be remembered, what would it be?

A Prayer
Almighty and most merciful God,
Out of the dust of the earth you created us,
Male and female you fashioned in your image.
Keep us ever mindful of the fragility of life,
And of its precious nature, of its glorious gift.
In your mercy forgive my moments of ingratitude,
Strengthen my resolve to open my life to your
Leading, to your power, to your presence,
That as my earthly days begin to fade with each
    passing moment,
I may not fear, but instead rest in
The blessed assurance of everlasting life with you,
And all the saints in light.
Through Christ our Lord.
Amen.

Sinning Business

For there is no distinction, since all have sinned and
fall short of the glory of God . . . .

—Romans 3:22–23

"I am a sinner." It's out; now you know.

I hate admitting it and, even worse, saying it aloud. But it is a
truth I cannot deny. I suppose if the Apostle Paul could admit it in
his letter to the Romans, I should be willing to do the same.

Over the years, I have presided at many religious services that
began by dawn's early light. Between the time I woke and the time
I found myself kneeling for the confession during those services,
there was hardly a chance to get to any sinning business. Yet, even
though I have spent the majority of my adult life in religious life, I
find that every time I kneel, my sin is staring me in the face. And
I realize that behind every confession the culprit is me!

I would like to think I am not too self-centered, but I do struggle
to not overfeed the one in the mirror. Perhaps we all do. When we
look at our photos, don't we look at ourselves first?

"How did I turn out?"

"Why did I wear that shirt?"

"I should have worn sunglasses."

After that, perhaps our eyes turn to our loved ones, our children, or the friend with whom we traveled. We are naturally drawn
to ourselves, and that is not all bad. We are to love ourselves, Jesus
said, but, at the same time he also told us to deny ourselves when
our "selves" get in the way of loving God or our neighbor.[2]

---

2   Luke 9:23; 10:27.

Life would be so much easier if all we had to do was carry out the "loving self" bit and let the rest alone. Too much self leads to one road and one road alone: sin in all of its forms. The overindulgent love of self is the thing the serpent said to the first humans "Eat and you will be like God."[3] The temptation was not to be the first in history to taste a Granny Smith, but the desire to "be like God." The appeal was to "put yourself on the throne and forget about God ruling your lives." How did it turn out? Read today's paper or watch the evening news and you can see what happens when we try to run things. Suddenly, taking on the role of God seems to be way above our pay grade.

Thus, we must still work on giving the "self" over to God in Christ more and more. Christians believe that is the only path to wholeness. It is why Jesus often described the whole journey of Christianity as starting with a kind of new birth. He called it being "born again."[4] For the fullness of God's presence to begin in me, "I" have to die and be "born anew." Please do not let those words alarm you. Use whatever metaphor works for you: "converted," "seeing the light," "renewed," or "awakened."

John Mason wrote, "They that deny themselves for Christ shall enjoy themselves in Christ."[5] The point is to deny ourselves and find our true selves, to allow the self to die and commence the life God wants for us. And that is a miracle to behold indeed. Perhaps it is time to get in touch with ourselves and see how much it might be getting in the way of the Godself that needs to be born in us.

— *Another Step . . .* —

What is the first selfish trait that is interfering in your relationship with God and others? Ask God to help you release it into His loving and redemptive care.

---

3 Genesis 3:5.
4 John 3:3.
5 Martin H. Manser, comp. *The Westminster Collection of Christian Quotations* (Louisville: Westminster John Knox, 2001), 335.

A Prayer

Lord Jesus, here I am, this mixed up tent of broken poles and torn fabric; this vessel with cracks and chips; this all-too-human and frail child of your own creation. And yet I have abused Your gift of life, taken advantage of the freedom You have awarded me, betrayed Your mercy once again. I have sinned, my heavenly Savior—in thought and word and deed, against You, my neighbor and myself. I have sinned deliberately, and I have sinned in ignorance; I have both chosen my sin and fallen into it. And now the burden of my wrong choices and the weight of their guilt is too much. Forgive me, dear Lord; forgive me and make me new. Empty me of all things impure and unholy, and fill me afresh with Your Holy Spirit that all broken places may be restored, and all sin be wiped away. Forgive me, O Lord, forgive me and make me new. *Amen.*

—RJL+

Do Over

"Very truly, I tell you, no one can see the kingdom of God without being born from above."

—John 3:3

When I was a kid, before the age of hyper-competitive children's sports, it was not uncommon to call for a "do over" on the ball field. What that meant in T-ball was that when the batter might have tapped the ball without intending to hit it, it was not to be counted against him as an attempt to smack it out of the park. He got to do it over. I rarely smacked it out of the park, but I was always grateful for a "do over"—a chance to give it another try without having my past mistakes counting against me.

In a well-known scene from John's gospel, Jesus met with a major religious leader named Nicodemus, who was a good and godly man. He knew his scriptures, practiced his religion, and was not afraid to spar with someone like Jesus. He was also spiritually hungry. All his attention to the rules of religion did not scratch his deeper spiritual itch. Jesus hit the nail on the head: "Very truly, I tell you, no one can see the kingdom of God without being born from above." Jesus wanted Nicodemus to see that his eyes and heart were focused on the Law and not the Lawgiver. Jesus told Nicodemus he needed a "do over."

He needed not just greater understanding, but new eyes, a new mind, a new heart, and a new self, which required a kind of internal, global shift in the tectonic plates of his being. He needed to be born again, as some biblical translations put it.

As I wrote in the previous meditation, don't let those two words frighten you. If you think on it long enough, who wouldn't want a "do over "in some area of life? The husband who has betrayed his wife? The employee who has stolen, or the employer who has treated workers harshly? The mother who has spent more time disciplining her children than loving and accepting them? The teenager caught in a web of alcohol or drug addiction? The criminal who acted in haste and without forethought? The friend who has neglected?

The opportunity for a "do over" is not limited to one event, but to our entire way of seeing things, and perhaps, even our entire life. The invitation Jesus issues to Nicodemus, and to each of us, is that new life finds its origin—its birthplace, if you will—not in religion, but in relationship. True religion is an expression of our relationship to God. Later in John's gospel, Jesus teaches that "all who see the Son and believe in him may have eternal life" (John 6:40). John Newton once said, "Christianity is not a system of doctrine but a new creature."

We all know we cannot change the past, but what Jesus always offers us is the opportunity to start afresh. The invitation to be born anew is more powerful than the simple permission for a "do over." It is the opportunity to have a whole new life—a life grounded not in stifling expectations of perfection, but in giving room for another try with God as our companion along the way.

— *Another Step . . .* —

What area of your life, past mistake, sin, or relationship would you like to do over? Can you offer that into the care of Christ who offers you new birth? Can you accept that gift?

A Prayer

O God, the King eternal, whose light divides the day from the night and turns the shadow of death into the morning: drive far from us all wrong desires, incline our hearts to keep your law, and guide our feet into the way of peace; that having done your will with cheerfulness during the day, we may, when night comes, rejoice to give you thanks; through Jesus Christ our Lord. *Amen.*

—William Reed Huntingdon, d. 1909[6]

---

6   Book of Common Prayer (New York: Church Hymnal Corporation, 1979), 56.

Forgive Us Our Sins . . .

"... forgive us our debts, as we also have forgiven our debtors."

—Matthew 6:12

When we ponder things like death and how we live our lives, it is not long before the issue of forgiveness rises to the surface.

For Jesus's earliest followers, to sin was to "miss the mark," much like an archer might fail to hit the bull's-eye. Sometimes an archer hits it dead on, but that is the exception and not the rule. We modern archers know we miss the mark most of the time. Many of our lives are peppered with the dark grains of sin. How then can forgiveness become more than a word?

From time to time I read of someone who boldly proclaims that the concept of a need for forgiveness is outdated. The modern mantra of "live as you please" taken to the extreme means there is no right and wrong, as long as you are happy with your life. But the longer we live, we find it is not hard to begin to feel what can only be described as a burden of guilt. In an interview with the BBC shortly before her death, well-known secular humanist Marghanita Laski said, "What I envy most about you Christians is your forgiveness; I have nobody to forgive me."[7]

John Claypool wrote, "You cannot ignore sin just because it is distasteful. Disposing of guilt by evasion is a way of dealing with it, but an utterly disastrous one; you might as well gather up the termites you find in the living room and deal with them by

---

7   John R. W. Stott, *The Contemporary Christian: Applying God's Word to Today's World* (New York: InterVarsity, 1995), 48.

turning them loose in your basement!"[8] How then do we begin to wrestle with forgiveness?

Christians affirm a kind of universal forgiveness offered in the death of Jesus Christ. It is hard to understand and even embrace for several reasons. Once we have gotten past the naïve belief that when we hurt others it really does not matter and there is no need for their forgiveness, then it is a human tendency to try to "pay up" for our mistakes. That is why in the Lord's Prayer, the request "forgive us" is sometimes accompanied by the word debt. A debt is something that has to be paid. But who pays it?

Perhaps one of the real misunderstandings about Christianity is that our acceptance by God is based on balancing some kind of great ledger. If the good marks outweigh the bad, then you pass the test (bull's-eye!), but if the bad outweigh the good, the trap door opens and down you go (you miss the mark). That kind of Christianity is not based on who you are, but on what you do. And if God's love depends on what we do, then we are no doubt already behind the curve. But if it is based on who we are, then there may just be a chance—if we understand who we are. And who are we?

In the last meditation we saw where Jesus brought it all home for Nicodemus with some words well known to Christians and non-Christians alike: "For God so loved the world that he gave his only Son, so that everyone who believes in him may not perish but may have eternal life. Indeed, God did not send the Son into the world to condemn the world, but in order that the world might be saved through him" (John 3:16–17). All of that love, life, non-condemnation, and promise of salvation business sounds more like a God who is offering forgiveness, does it not?

So where do we take our sins? I take them to the Cross of Jesus Christ. On the Cross, Jesus was willing to absorb all the evil, sin, and guilt of the world; he was willing to take them on himself. Theologians call this "substitutionary atonement," meaning the atonement that might be paid through any other form is

---

8   John Claypool, *The Light Within You: Looking at Life Through New Eyes* (Waco, TX: Word Books, 1983), 186.

transferred, substituted by a stand-in: Jesus Christ. That is why Jesus's first cousin, John the Baptist, called him "the Lamb of God who takes away the sin of the world!" (John 1:29).

Perhaps the place to begin understanding forgiveness is to give up some old misconceptions about it: that we somehow pay the price for our own sins, that forgiveness is unnecessary, or that God is more like a celestial accountant than a heavenly parent. I will unpack this more in the pages to come, but for now, let go of the Divine Accountant and let the Loving God take hold of you.

— *Another Step . . .* —

When you read or hear the word "guilt," what first comes to mind? And the word "forgiveness"?

A Prayer

O My Lord, since it seems you are determined
to save me, I ask that you may do so quickly.
And since you have decided to dwell within me,
I ask that you clean your house, wiping away all
grime of sin.

—Teresa of Avila, d. 1582

... As We Forgive Those Who Sin Against Us

Then Peter came and said to Him, "Lord, if another member of the church sins against me, how often should I forgive? As many as seven times?" Jesus said to him, "Not seven times, but, I tell you, seventy times seven."

—Matthew 18:21–22

In some ways, this scene between Peter and Jesus is comical. Anyone who has had to deal with children has probably encountered the crying child trying to justify his or her naughty behavior with the words, "They did it first!" No doubt, Peter was trying to find some way of wiggling out of forgiving even one more time. And yet, Jesus does not let him off the hook. "You are not to forgive just seven times, but seventy times seven!" As you may know, in Jesus's day, seven was a symbol, not just a number. It often had an eternal, endless quality to it. So really, Jesus is not telling Peter that forgiveness runs out after the four hundred and ninetieth time, but to forgive and forgive and forgive.

Why should we do that? One reason is clear. Jesus tells us to pray, "Forgive us our sins as we forgive those who sin against us."[9] If we do not forgive others, we lock God's forgiveness out of our own hearts. If we deny forgiveness, we allow our pain to give way to anger, resentment, and even hatred, festering within us like

---

9   Matthew 6:12.

a poison. Frederick Buechner writes about anger's effect on the human soul:

> Of the Seven Deadly Sins, anger is possibly the most fun. To lick your wounds, to smack your lips over grievances long past, to roll over your tongue the prospect of bitter confrontations still to come, to savor to the last toothsome morsel—both the pain you are given and the pain you are giving back—in many ways it is a feast fit for a king. The chief drawback is that what you are wolfing down is yourself. The skeleton at the feast is you.[10]

At this point, it may be tempting to allow the "Yes, buts" to gather.

"Yes, but can we forgive if our enemy does not repent?" Jesus might answer, "Can your enemy repent unless you are willing to forgive?" On the Cross, Jesus prayed that his enemies might be forgiven while they were still intent on his death.

"Yes, but you don't know how badly I have been hurt." That may be true. It might be that we do not know how badly we have hurt your offender. Nevertheless, we pray, "Forgive us our sins, as we forgive those who sin against us."

"Yes, but what if we forgive and they hurt us again?" Jesus says forgive "seventy times seven." If we want to experience the healing power of mercy, we must be willing to shell it out. Our other choice is to let all the pain, wounds, and resentment continue to have power over us.

Offering forgiveness is freeing. How long do you want the words anger, resentment, or grudge to be part of our heart's vocabulary? Better to let them go so that not only have we given mercy, but we have made room in our lives for it to enter in as well.

---

10 Frederick Buechner, *Wishful Thinking: A Theological ABC* (San Francisco: Harper & Row, 1973), 2.

— *Another Step . . .* —
Who do you need to forgive today? Why are you waiting?

A Prayer
O Lord, remember not only the men and women of
good will, but also those of ill will. But do not remember all the suffering they have inflicted on us;
remember the fruits we have bought, thanks to this
suffering—our comradeship, our loyalty, our courage, our generosity, the greatness of heart which has
grown out of all of this, and when they come to judgment let all the fruits which we have borne be their
forgiveness.

—This prayer was written by an unknown
prisoner at Ravensbruck Concentration
Camp and left by the body of a dead child[11]

11 Mary Batchelor, comp. *The Doubleday Prayer Collection* (New York: Doubleday, 1997), 50–51.

...As We Forgive Ourselves

...as far as the east is from the west, so far he removes our transgressions from us.

—Psalm 103:12

Having touched on forgiveness in general, that is the need to seek forgiveness by saying "I am sorry" and the need to forgive others by extending mercy, we have one more "directional" imperative to consider: forgiving ourselves.

That concept may seem a bit out of place. If we have sought forgiveness from God, is it not God's business, and not ours, to forgive? Well, yes and no. God does seek to forgive and God does forgive. As noted in the Psalm above, God's forgiveness takes our wrongdoing and flings it as far as the east is from the west. If we are earnest and give our sins to God, God wipes them away. We may still have to live with the consequences of our sins, but God will not hold them over us. But just because God has forgiven us, that does not mean we have forgiven ourselves.

Guilt is a helpful tool at times. It can bring us to our knees pleading for the mercy of God when we need it. But once God has forgiven us, we need to let go of our guilt. If it sticks around, it is not of God. It can drive us down into despair, into a feeling of unworthiness such that we do not even want to be in the presence of God.

One of my closest friends, a psychiatrist, was having lunch with a colleague who was the administrator of an inpatient mental health facility. He told my friend, "You know, if I could ever get two messages into the psyche and heart of each of these patients,

I could release most of them today: you are forgiven and you are loved."

"Forgive us our sins, as we forgive ourselves" is perhaps the last step we take in dealing with our personal sin and its traveling companion, guilt. However, there is another good reason to learn to accept God's forgiveness. We will also learn to spend less time on how "I" feel all the time, and more time on how others feel. Accepting forgiveness allows us to be more merciful to others.

Forgive us our sins, as we seek forgiveness, as we forgive others, and as we forgive ourselves. What has God chosen to do with the sin we have brought to him for forgiveness? God has forgiven us. Why should we not do the same?

— *Another Step . . .* —

Take some time and reflect on God's forgiveness. Receive it—not just for a moment, but for all the days ahead.

A Prayer

Lord Jesus, you taught us to forgive others, just as you forgave those who treated you badly. Help us to remember how much you have forgiven us and to be willing to forgive those who hurt us. For your sake, Amen.

—A children's prayer[12]

---

12 Edna and Jack Young, *Praying with Juniors* (Surrey, UK: National Christian Education Council, 1968).

The Burnt-Over Place

Out of his anguish he shall see light; he shall find sat-
isfaction through his knowledge. The righteous one,
my servant, shall make many righteous, and he shall
bear their iniquities.

—Isaiah 53:11

A clergy friend of mine told me of a time when two of his church
members were duck hunting in South Georgia. They were trapped
by the onset of a fast-moving brushfire. They saw no means of
escape until one of them came up with an idea. He took a match
and started a much smaller fire around them. After a few minutes,
the two of them were sitting in the middle of a black circle where
the brush under their feet had already been burned. They cov-
ered their mouths with wet cloths and waited for the oncoming
blaze. The runaway fire moved right around them; fire cannot
pass where things have already burned.

Among Isaiah's many writings are included several images of
the "Suffering Servant," foreshadowing the death of Jesus for the
sin of all humankind. Jesus's act of making sinful people righteous
is called *justification*. What it means in practical terms is that
Jesus burned a circle around us so the fire of sin will not consume
us. We are justified. Reconciled. Made right with God through
Jesus's burning love on the Cross. That does not mean we are free
from the consequences of our sin. Forgiveness of the tax cheat
by God does not mean they will not have to deal with the IRS.
Forgiveness of the adulterer by God does not mean that the pain
of the offended will be wiped away, and so on. No, justification in

God's eyes means simply that in the last court of appeal, the gavel's fall comes with the two words, "Not guilty."

The Cross of Christ, the death of the Suffering Servant, is that "burned-over" place. Punishment cannot be revisited in a place where punishment has already occurred. When we come to terms with that, there is a real freedom in knowing that while we may still have to deal with some of the earthly consequences of our sinful behavior like confession, reconciliation, and restitution, in God's eyes there is nothing left to burn. We are forgiven.

— *Another Step . . .* —

What things do you do to try to win God's justification? If you have been justified by Jesus's death on the Cross, what more can you do than be thankful? Take some time and offer that thanks.

A Prayer

O God, before Whose face we are not made
righteous even by being right; free us from the
need to justify ourselves by our own anxious
striving, that we may be abandoned to faith in
you alone, through Jesus Christ. *Amen.*

—RJL+

The Waiting Game

Wait for the Lord; be strong, and let your heart take courage; wait for the Lord!

—Psalm 27:14

I have spent a good bit of this particular day waiting. I waited on the cable guy to come and fix our connection. I waited on the electrician to repair some outlets that had stopped working. On the way to the doctor I had to wait in traffic and when I arrived at the doctor's office, I waited some more.

Waiting is hard for us in our industrialized, immediate, internet world. We have invented ways to fill up the dead space of waiting. We check our smartphones while waiting at red lights. We check e-mail or Facebook to pass the time.

Our Judeo-Christian faith is centered around waiting. In the opening chapters of Genesis, the first real outcome of Adam's disobedience was he would no longer have food at the snap of his fingers; he would have to toil the land "by the sweat of your face."[13] In other words, he would have to learn to wait for what he wanted.

The history of Judaism is wrapped up in waiting for the Messiah. Moses spent forty years waiting in the desert before he could lead the Jews into the Promised Land. Jesus spent forty days waiting in the desert before he began his ministry. Once Jesus came, the history of Christians became, and remains, focused on waiting for his return.

Waiting is difficult. Waiting on the exam grades to be posted. Waiting on the call after the job interview. Waiting for the

---

13 Genesis 3:17–19.

wedding to be over. Waiting for the baby to arrive. Waiting on the diagnosis. Waiting for the pain to stop. The "waiting game" though is much fun.

There are, however, at least two ways to learn to live with waiting. The first is to settle into it. Any physician would tell us that to stop and take a breather is a good thing for our physical health. The same is true of our spiritual health. When circumstances cause us to stop—to wait—we can use that time to think on the days gone by, the moment we are in, or the things yet to come. We can pray for others—for the man in traffic next to you, the woman in line in front of you; we can pray for ourselves.

The second way to play the waiting game is to embrace what it may be all about—turning more to God. David's words in Psalm 27 are a poem to his reader, but perhaps also to himself. He had enemies galore and wanted protection. He did not want God to forget him. He had to wait, and when he did, he also realized that he was waiting *on the Lord*. David's inability to control his own situation, to speed things up or end the waiting game, *made him turn to God*.

Maybe waiting is not all that bad. Maybe it is a gift sent from God; a gift to give us a bit more time to think, pray, rest, or prepare. Maybe it is a gift from a sender who wants us to turn our hearts back to him because our busy schedules and chiming devices make it difficult for us to be still enough to listen.

Maybe waiting is a gift. Just *wait* a minute. No, really.

— *Another Step . . .* —

When you are made to wait today, as you probably will be, how can you fill that time in a way that responds to David's words, "Wait for the Lord"?

A Prayer

You keep us waiting.
You, the God of all time,
Want us to wait
For the right time in which to discover
Who we are, where we must go,
Who will be with us, and what we must do.
So, thank you . . . for the waiting time.

—A prayer of *The Iona Community*

Being Sure of What We Do Not See

Now faith is the assurance of things hoped for, the conviction of things not seen.

—Hebrews 11:1

As I write this, my wife and I are preparing to move to a home that is closer to my office, which will make life more manageable, we hope. As a result, I am caught up in all the business and the busyness of the move: securing the financing, figuring out where the furniture will fit, and managing the renovation budget.

A great deal of life feels like busy work, does it not? We can become consumed with our careers, planning for retirement, figuring out how to send the kids to college, or how to pay for the next car. Maybe we lose time pondering old wounds and grudges of the past. Some of us are doing all we can to stay afloat: "How will I pay that bill?" "How can I face the person I cannot stand one more day?" "How can I undergo one more treatment?"

Now not all of these things are bad. Many of them are important things to which we must tend, but they are not the most important things. What matters most are the things that we cannot necessarily see or prove, but we believe and live: the power of prayer, in the necessity of holiness, the demands of love, the truths of redemption, mercy, grace, and resurrection. These are all gifts of faith, as the Bible says, outgrowths of being sure of things we cannot really see.

Our world is full of superficial spirituality. I remember going through the grocery store checkout line some time ago and seeing an issue of *Self* magazine (a sign of our times). It was a special "Spirituality" issue. I couldn't resist. Among the several articles, most of them brief, I found Spiritual Workouts, The Ten Commandments for Today, and perhaps my favorite, Spiritual Fashion.

We can find articles on the spirituality of aromatherapy or watch morning talk show segments on the power of reading Whitman in the hot tub. When a pop star whose lyrics are laced with profanity receives an award, they seem to always grab the cross around their neck and thank God—along with their producer and publicist. Some see Christianity in the same light. It is generally a good thing. Church is a nice place to go because it is healthy, like a good workout or a day at the spa.

But let us be honest. Even though candles, music, and even good wine can enhance spirituality, their depth of spirituality is equal to eye shadow—easily applied, easily removed. A skin-deep spirituality shows up in shallow life commitments. A sporting event on the weekend takes precedence over our worship with God. A late-night party edges out the need to close our day in prayer. The demands of the working world keep us from studying the scriptures. Our financial commitments to the work of Christ slowly creep to the bottom of the list after things like a new plasma screen, a weekend in Vegas, or new furniture for the guest room.

In his second letter to Timothy, the apostle Paul put shallow spirituality and cotton-candy theology in their place. Paul gave up everything for the gospel: his reputation, his status, his friends, and his wealth. And where do we find him? Bound in chains during the Neronian persecution, languishing in a dungeon, abandoned and awaiting execution. He was about to follow in the footsteps of all but two of Jesus's apostles into martyrdom. Paul, at this point, had lost everything temporal. He was, at the end, like all of the great early Christians, fighting against the empty vessel of the material world. His gospel was not grounded in the world of touch, taste, or smell. He wrote, "As for me, I am already being poured out as a libation, and the time of my departure has come. I have fought the good fight, I have finished the race, I have kept the faith" (2 Timothy 4:6–7).

Some of the last words Paul ever wrote were not "Look at where I am," but rather, "Look at where I am going." Paul's words reflected what Jesus demanded: the one who gives up their life saves it, not the other way around.

A true spirituality that is grounded in the self-sacrificial commitment to Christ pinches, pokes, and probes at our need to come down off our high horses and humbly fall on our faces before the God of the universe, who gives us life. Thus, we throw off everything that gets in the way—each and every distraction. If we do not, our spirituality is as shallow as a spring puddle that dries up with the first rays of sun.

Join me in rereading Paul's words. "As for me, I am already being poured out as a libation, and the time of my departure has come. I have fought the good fight, I have finished the race, I have kept the faith." And that faith, as the writer of Hebrews says, is something we can "be sure of but cannot see."

— *Another Step . . .* —

Spend a moment and think on that temporal thing to which you are clinging just a bit too tightly today. How can you loosen your grip, or perhaps, let go altogether?

A Prayer
Take, Lord, as your right, and receive as my gift,
all my freedom, my memory, my mind and my
will. Whatever I am and whatever I possess,
you have given to me; I give it all back to you.
Dispose of me, and the powers you gave me,
according to your will. Give me only a love for
you, and the gift of your grace; then I am rich
enough, and ask for nothing more.
—St. Ignatius Loyola, d. 1556[14]

14 Michael Counsell, comp. *2000 Years of Prayer* (Harrisburg, PA: Morehouse, 1999), 204.

A Time for Everything

For everything there is a season, and a time for every matter under heaven: a time to be born, a time to die; a time to plant, and a time to pluck up what is planted; . . . a time to weep, and a time to laugh; a time to mourn, and a time to dance . . . .

—Ecclesiastes 3:1–2, 4

One morning, I was looking out at my yard and I remembered a swing set that we had torn down shortly after we moved in. At least for now, we are out of the "swing set" season of life. A tiny bit of melancholy set in as I thought of the many swing sets in the many yards we have had over our quarter-century of marriage.

My wife and I have lived in nearly a dozen homes in six different states. Every move has required us to offer our hellos and good-byes. If walls could talk, each home could speak of uproarious laughter and quiet tears, parental discipline and praise, parties with full rooms of guests and quiet evenings in front of the fire. Every carpet held the stains of morning coffee that sat with us through quiet times of prayer and study, and wine that tipped over the edge of a glass during a movie or a night with friends. We had a garage sale in every home, and then some good-serving nonprofit organization came by to pick up the leftovers. Recently, we let go of a chest of drawers my wife owned for over thirty years and a desk I have had since I was five.

Change rarely comes without difficulty, and when it comes, there is absolutely nothing we can do about it. We can do something in anticipation of it, which is to welcome it. My wife and I could have resisted all the little (and big) changes that came with our life, but we would have missed so much of the experience of life itself.

Some are thrilled with the opportunity to begin again and embrace it. Many others worry about saying good-bye because they don't know what the hello of the future holds. Depending on the situation, we know how it feels to be on either side. Whatever the circumstance, we cannot hold so fast to the past that we cannot, with joy and hope, embrace the good things that may come with the future.

When that swing set was moved out, it left room for a horseshoe pit and lawn enough for some small football games. Perhaps on another day it will be a meditation garden to sit and talk with growing children. That does not mean the swing set was not a good thing; it was just time for a different thing, a different season.

I finished up this little pondering with an afternoon run. I do not run as far as I used to, but as I wound it up, I passed one of my senior neighbors on an afternoon walk with his cane. My guess is in a season still to come, I will be out walking with my cane and a younger man will pass me on his afternoon run.

Change is inevitable. What we hope to hold in the present becomes the past and opens the door to the future. Life is its own little roller-coaster ride. Whatever this day may bring, or what may change tomorrow, we must live in the season of the present, which is best done when we are willing to enjoy the ride. Our ups and downs are made enjoyable and more manageable in Christ. "[He] is the same yesterday and today and forever" (Hebrews 13:8)—whatever the season or the change.

—— *Another Step . . .* ——

What change are you anticipating in the season ahead? How can you best welcome it into your life?

A Prayer

Be present, O merciful God, and protect us through the silent hours of this night, so that we who are wearied by the changes and chances of this fleeting world may repose upon your eternal changelessness; through Jesus Christ our Lord. *Amen.*

—Pope Leo the Great, d. 461[15]

---

15 Book of Common Prayer, 133.

Time Will Tell

And not only that, but we also boast in our suffer-
ings, knowing that suffering produces endurance,
and endurance produces character, and character
produces hope, and hope does not disappoint us,
because God's love has been poured into our hearts
through the Holy Spirit that has been given to us.

—Romans 5:3–5

"Only time will tell" is one of those quotes that is, frankly, sometimes helpful and sometimes irritating. My grandmother used
to say it a great deal when imploring "patience" from her grands
about a wide variety of things. It is not a bad quote to tug on, particularly when we are moving through a dark period in life when
pain and suffering feel unbearable. In the long term, things often
look different and can be interpreted differently. In the moment
of childbirth, a soon-to-be mother doesn't ponder the joy of par-
enting. A struggling parent rarely ponders the long view of a pro-
ductive young adult. In the midst of graduate school, the budding
law student or medical student struggles to become someone who
can make a positive difference in the world. In the gym, weights
curled and hurled rarely produce strong muscles without some
pain. You get the picture.

But why on earth does pain have to be part of the recipe of
human existence? Let me answer in two parts. First of all, we
rarely think in terms of the long range. We are too often bound to
a twenty-four-hour clock. We tend to live minute by minute, hour
by hour, day by day. An addict in a thirty-day recovery program
would likely prefer to be fixed overnight, but it does not work that

way. We want our prayers answered now, but we tend to forget that God is not bound by time. God is literally outside the limits of time. We have to unchain ourselves from the clock when it comes to dealing with God's time and ours.

Astronomers tell us that when we look up at a faraway star, our eyes are taking in light from millions of years before. That star may have long ago exploded and yet, to us, it is glowing in the present moment.

Physicist Stephen Hawking has quoted Augustine's belief that any god must exist outside of time. The theory of relativity has been proven with experiments that show time is not bound by our clock. For instance, if an astronaut could travel at the speed of light, time would actually slow down for them. When they returned to earth, they would be younger than someone of the same age who had stayed on earth. That is hard to understand because we are so bound by time. But if we can realize God works outside of our sense of time, perhaps it is easier to consider that our momentary pains might be doing something good that we cannot now imagine—which leads me to the second part of my recipe.

The best way I know to sum this up is found in the passage from Romans on the first page of this meditation. Paul tells us something about the tether connecting the passage of time with our pain that makes us more than we thought we could be. I would love to say it is easier than that, but let that explanation settle in just a moment. If you have experienced the pain of childbirth, would you give up that pain if it also meant giving up your child? If you have experienced the trials of maintaining a strong friendship or marriage, would you let go of that pain if it meant a life of loneliness? If you have experienced a measure of inner peace after a long period on your knees, would you give up that peace? If you are one who does know what it means to have a relationship with God, you also know you must continue to give up, surrender your own life into His hands. Would you pass up that life for keeping yourself to yourself?

"No pain, no gain" sounds really nifty at the gym, but it is not as much fun when we are moving through the personal pain of a

struggling marriage, another chemo treatment, an estranged relationship with a child, a divided community of faith, and any other
pain of existence. But there is some truth to that bumper sticker
philosophy. Aleksandr Solzhenitsyn wrote of his own experience
with the trials of pain over time

> It was only when I lay there on rotting prison straw that
> I sensed within myself the first stirrings of good. Grad-
> ually, it was disclosed to me that the line separating
> good and evil passes, not through states, nor between
> classes, nor between political parties either—but right
> through all human hearts. . . . So, bless you, prison, for
> having been in my life.[16]

His words respond to both pieces of my recipe. It was not in
the moment, but in looking at the "whole" of the moment, that
a greater understanding about human nature and relationship to
God became clearer and made sense to him. While he might have
liked to have come to this realization in a different way, it was the
suffering in prison that brought about that clarity.

I do not know what suffering you may be going through at this
very moment, but I echo the words of Corrie Ten Boom: "[T]here
is no pit so deep that He is not deeper still."[17] That kind of truth
is often not clear in the moment. We need the gift of perspective,
of being outside of time. When my own moments of anguish were
over, I began to find clarity, meaning, and even purpose in what
had happened; it was not until much later that I could even begin
to see God's hand.

I cannot say that every mystery around pain and suffering has
yet to be revealed in my own journey. I still have lots of questions.
You may as well. So, I guess my grandmother's words still are true,
"Only time will tell."

---

16 Aleksandr I. Solzhenitsyn, *The Gulag Archipelago 1918–1956* (New York: Harper Perennial
    Modern Classics, 2002), 312–313.
17 Corrie Ten Boom, *The Hiding Place* (Grand Rapids: Chosen Books, 2007), 227.

⎯ *Another Step . . .* ⎯

If you are experiencing some pain in your life right now, take some time to reflect on how that pain, over time, may strengthen you more than you are now. Is there anything good that has come out of this time of pain?

A Prayer

O God, as I travel through this pain, this trial, this struggle, be present, be present, O my strength and salvation. I pray for the end of this season of suffering that accords with Your purpose and refinement of my soul. If that pain ends now, give me a grateful heart for its relief and whatever has been gained. If its end is beyond my time of yearning, then give me power to endure, character to receive, and hope to carry me to its perfect end. *Amen.*

—RJL+

Taste and See

O taste and see that the Lord is good . . . .

—Psalm 34:8

Not too long ago, work called me away from a televised tennis match that was reaching a nail-biting conclusion. Fortunately, I had a DVR, so I recorded it. I was out rather late and made a point of avoiding any news outlets that might announce the winner. The next morning I woke, grabbed my morning coffee, flipped on the television, and hit *Play* on the remote. At times, I almost could not stand the suspense. I was tempted just to fast-forward to see how it turned out, but something in me said, "No, you'll spoil the match if you reveal the winner too early."

Many of us would like a fast-forward button in our lives. When the doctor calls with bad news, we would love to fast-forward to see how it all turns out. When the boss gives a bad review, the police station calls to say they have one of ours in custody, the stock market takes a turn for the worse, or there is an envelope with a legal office return address, we would love to fast-forward to see what happens. The same is true for good news. When the tax return envelope comes, a child graduates, we meet someone who may just be that "special" someone, or the boss calls offering a promotion, we want to fast-forward.

But if we hit the fast-forward button, whether in anticipation of bad news or good, we miss the adventure in between. And believe it or not, there is often adventure in that "in betweenness" of waiting for the end of the story.

In the world in which we live, so much gets lost in the rush of all the busy-ness. We tend, in all this rushing about, to forget to hit a much more important button than fast-forward: the pause button. I do not believe our God gave us our lives so we could speed up and miss the enjoyment of the ride.

When I was young, my father and I often frequented a bar-beque spot in my native city of Birmingham, Alabama. The owner had posted the above verse, "Taste and see," on a large plaque over his smoking BBQ pits. As a Christian, it was his way of reminding his patrons that the gift of food was not to be wolfed down, but eaten slowly, savored, enjoyed. God's gifts of our senses are also a reminder to enjoy, to take it all in.

I once saw a one-woman play entitled *The Golden Egg.* It began with a little girl who was frustrated with a situation at school, and she wished that she could go on to the next grade. An old mystic appeared and gave her a golden egg with a small piece of string hanging out. The mystic told the little girl that any time she ran into a painful, uncomfortable situation, pull on the string and time would fly.

The little girl snatched out a section of string and found herself in the next grade. But moving forward faster and faster was too much of a temptation. Every time she ran into something she didn't like, she yanked on that string. Sometimes she pulled too hard. Not wanting to wait for her wedding, she yanked, but then she missed her honeymoon. When labor pains came, another yank, but she missed her baby's first smile and step. When her husband became ill, she pulled that string and she missed his death. She was just standing at his grave. She finally realized what she had done and tried to back up by sticking the string back into the egg. She could not; time really had flown.

Each and every day is precious, as are the moments and the relationships given to us as part of God's gift of life. Enjoy the extra time. Hold hands a bit longer, cuddle a bit more, watch the credits, or sleep a little later. Turn off the smart phone and hit the pause button every chance you get. And if not the pause button, then at least the play button. Steer clear of the fast-forward. Why? Taste and see! Taste and see!

—   *Another Step . . .*   —

How might you consciously hit the pause button this day?
Why not give it a try?

A Prayer

Lord, I have time
I have plenty of time,
All the time that you give me,
The years of my life,
The days of my years,
The hours of my days,
They are all mine.
Mine to fill, quietly, calmly,
But to fill completely, up to the brim,
To offer them to you, that of their insipid water
You may make a rich wine
such as you made once in Cana of Galilee.

—Michel Quoist[18]

---

18 Michel Quoist, *Prayers of Life* (Dublin: Gill & Macmillan, 1963).

Look at the Birds

"Look at the birds of the air; they neither sow nor reap nor gather into barns, and yet your heavenly Father feeds them. Are you not of more value than they?"

—Matthew 6:26

"Let the little birds be your theologians" is a thought attributed to Martin Luther. Not a bad suggestion. In his sermon on the mount, Jesus said, "Look at the birds of the air."

I have learned a lot from birds over the years. I once considered a vocation in ornithology, but preferred people over our feathered friends. However, I am still a novice bird watcher. We have feeders in our little backyard that attract blue jays, sparrows, finches, blackbirds, cowbirds, doves of a few varieties, and two of the three predominant woodpeckers in the area of Texas where I live.

The other day I saw something I have never seen in all my years of "looking at the birds of the air." You probably know the sound a baby bird makes when it is following its mama bird about, waiting for food. A high-pitched squeak comes out of the stretched open beak. The baby often bounces and flutters its wings until the mother places a worm, a piece of seed, or a scrap of bread into the hungry mouth. If it is a really hungry bird, this can go on for an hour or more and the sound can get a bit on the nerves.

On this particular day, I heard that squeaking outside of my bedroom window for some time and finally decided to take a peek. Much to my surprise, I found a small brown cowbird hopping behind a bright red male cardinal. Something had gotten turned around. This baby was not following around its mama, but it was following around another bird's papa—and not even of the same species. I was fascinated to see what the male bird would do because that babe was not letting up as it bounced around right on the heels of its adopted dad. Then to my surprise, the pop picked up a bit of food and delivered it into the beak of his adopted child, not once, but at least twice.

Though this goes against what we think we know as the paternal nature of animals, it is not that unusual for one bird to take another into its care. However, I had never seen it with my own eyes. It made me wonder if I am that attentive to the open mouths I may pass by every day.

We all know our expected responsibilities: parents care for children, friends care for friends, work colleagues support and encourage one another. What about being especially attentive to those in need around us even when we are not, by nature or habit, driven or drawn to care for them? Are we aware of the "open beaks" we encounter every day? Do we realize that God may have allowed that someone to cross our path because we have it in us to care for them? And do we then, in turn, do what God hopes we will do?

Jesus suggested caring for others was one way of reaching out to him, ". . . just as you did it to one of the least of these who are members of my family, you did it to me" (Matthew 25:40). Sometimes that means visiting the sick, feeding the hungry, and clothing the naked. Sometimes it may mean just being a bit kinder to that checkout lady, the bag boy, the gas station attendant, or the person in traffic. It may be as simple as a smile or as intense as a visit to the ICU. I do know there are lots of little birds out there who may be waiting for us to step outside of what is expected and care when there is no one else who can.

So, let the little birds be your theologians. If a cardinal can care for one that is not his own, surely we can do the same. May we have eyes to see that Jesus was right, "Look at the birds . . . ."

— *Another Step...* —
Watch today and tomorrow. See if there is someone in your path who needs something only you can give. Watch.

A Prayer
Make us true servants to all those in need,
Filled with compassion in thought, word and deed;
Loving our neighbor, whatever the cost,
Feeding the hungry and finding the lost.
Lord, make us healers of body and mind;
Give us your power to bring sight to the blind;
Love to the loveless and gladness for pain,
Filling all hearts with the joy of your name.

—Susan G. Wente[19]

---

19 From the song, *Make Us True Servants.*

Pure Religion

Religion that is pure and undefiled before God, the Father, is this: to care for orphans and widows in their distress, and to keep oneself unstained by the world.

—James 1:27

Every now and then, someone asks me to "sum up" Christianity. That is no small order, but I can cite verses like this one to help me point the way. James was writing to the early Christian community who had gotten just a bit too heavy on the "faith" side of things, without translating their faith in the practice of loving deeds. Evidently those in James's particular audience had forgotten some of the orphans and widows in their care. They had gotten too caught up in their "stained by the world," as it were, which had about as many opportunities to be corrupt as our own.

One of the earliest heresies of the church was called Gnosticism. Now I could write pages, even volumes on this heresy, but one key element was the belief that somehow there was no real connection between one's soul and one's body. Thus, you could "believe" as a follower of Christ, but your body was so corrupt that it could not possibly be expected to be good. It was easy, then, for Gnostics to (a) move into Christian communities because they shared many beliefs of the early Christian communities, but then (b) become somewhat bipartisan when it came to living out their faith in deeds.

That is why James smacks them upside the head (one of my favorite Southern expressions, by the way) with a reality check. "Hey! Don't forget, pure religion is a matter of the head and the heart, faith and deeds. So don't be so heavenly good that you are no earthly good. Don't have your head in the clouds and your body in the brothel."

James's clear directive is a general reflection of Jesus's primary command that the essence of our faith is "love of God and love of neighbor."[20] It is the giving of ourselves to God in Christ through confession and repentance of sin, a total offering of ourselves to the forgiveness offered by Jesus's death on the Cross and his rising to life again. The end result is a total conversion of the individual, body and soul. It is living out that conversion by a consistent pattern of confession, repentance, renewal, and conversion such that we begin to share the gospel through evangelism, bringing others to Jesus Christ, and through loving deeds as found in the care of others, charity, social justice, and societal change. Pure religion is a "combo meal" of committing ourselves to care for others and committing ourselves to God in Christ. For James that meant (a) caring for widows and orphans, and (b) keeping oneself from being defiled by the world.

I think that is a good pointer toward the essence of the faith. It would be easy to get so lost in our Christian duties that we forget we are also called to be faithful in living moral lives. I have seen many a Christian worker who has forgotten that part of the call to the Christian life—a call to goodness, purity, and morality. I once had a good friend who oversaw a shelter for the community. He was doing wonderful work. I later learned that when it came to ethical practices in the business of his shelter, his record was deplorable. He seemed to think that because he was doing good in the community, it really did not matter what his means were. The end result was the total collapse of his ministry.

I have also seen those who became so caught up in keeping pure from the stains of the world that they refused to interact with those they deemed just a bit too stained to endure. How does that measure up with a Lord and Savior who spent some of His best

---

20 Matthew 22:37–39.

work among prostitutes, winebibbers, tax collectors, and sinners? It does not.

No, the answer is to walk both lines—caring and personal holiness. These are hard lines to walk. We all stumble, but that is why some lines are drawn to help show us the way. Getting sidetracked? Why not read James's words once more, "Religion that is pure and undefiled before God, the Father, is this: to care for orphans and widows in their distress, and to keep oneself unstained by the world." Better yet, read Jesus's words as you find them in Matthew 22:37–39. And when you do, get to it.

— *Another Step . . .* —

As James places this mark of finding a way to walk faithfully between faith and deeds before you, how does it challenge you to step more deeply in your faith? To act more faithfully in your deeds?

A Prayer

Almighty God, in whom we live and move and have our being, you have made us for yourself, so that our hearts are restless till they rest in you; grant us purity of heart and strength of purpose, that no passion may hinder us from knowing your will, no weakness from doing it; but in your light may we see light clearly, and in your service find perfect freedom; through Jesus Christ our Lord, *Amen.*

—St. Augustine, d. 430[21]

---

21   Counsell, *2000 Years of Prayer*, 30.

God's Tattoo

... when Israel sought for rest, the Lord appeared
to him from far away, I have loved you with an everlasting love; therefore I have continued my faithfulness to you.

—Jeremiah 31:2–3

There are many things that have changed in my over half-cen-
tury of life; one of those is the tattoo. When I was a kid, if you
got a tattoo—which, by the way, was taboo in my home—you
really stood out of the crowd. Some sailors and military men got
tattoos, but rare was the occasion that a youth or teen followed
their lead. A visit to the beach or a trip to the gym tells me that
to really stand out from the crowd now, perhaps you ought not
get a tattoo.

I am not anti-tattoo, but I do think it is getting a bit silly. I
loved a little cartoon I saw not too long ago, showing a young
teen getting what she thought was a "hip" tattoo band around her
bicep. The next frame showed her years later as a grandmother,
with the band now down to her wrist. Her grandchild says, "Gee,
Grandma, you are really cool," at which point the grandma rolls
her eyes.

At our home, we recently heard the story of a man who had
the name of his wife tattooed within a heart-shaped design on his
chest. As children came along, he began putting their names in
as well. At the birth of the last, the tattoo artist actually got the
name wrong—something the man did not notice until it was all
over. So, what to do? They changed the name of the child to match
the mistake.

The Bible tells us about God's only tattoo. The prophet Isaiah describes it as he speaks of God's love for his children: "I will not forget you. See, I have inscribed you on the palms of my hands . . ." (Isaiah 49:15–16). Another translation says, "I have engraved you on the palm of my hand." God looks into God's hand, and there are our names.

Can you see that? Though metaphor for sure, can you see that as God sees that? We are constantly part of God's thinking. God's love is unwaning, secure, and endless. God does not have our names wrong or our faces. God's love in an indelible mark.

The verse at the start from Jeremiah is a bit different from much of the rest of his work. For most of his writing, Jeremiah was all about doom and gloom, but in this passage he allows those clouds to disperse just a bit to tell Israel that God loves them with an everlasting love. The Hebrew word was *hesed*, and it means "steadfast." In other words, there is nothing in heaven or on earth that could take God's love away. A constant, biding, immortal love—like a tattoo on our hearts—is what God has for us.

On the Cross, Jesus followed God's lead, and our names were "engraved" on his hands. These same hands of love welcomed rugged iron nails to say that his love for us was more precious than any other chapter of the story we know as the "universe."

God's love is an unerasable tattoo. May we rest, this day, in the security of that love.

— *Another Step . . .* —

God's love for you is higher and deeper than any love you have ever experienced. How does resting in that knowledge change the way you will face the day ahead?

A Prayer

Everlasting Father, you tell me that you love me
with an everlasting, steadfast, immortal love—
that my name is written on the palm of your
mighty hand. Free me, I pray, from the chatter
of noises that rob me of the experience of that
love—my own doubt and fear, anxieties and
worries, inadequacy and insecurity. Help me to
hear, once again, the whisper of your unbound-
ed love for me, that in the security of that love,
I may, in return, love you and all you send my
way. *Amen.*

—RJL+

Abundant Life

I came that they may have life, and have it abundantly.

—John 10:10

As a young boy, Frank Lloyd Wright was out walking in the snow one day with his father. They had traveled a bit in a rural area when his father stopped him and said, "Frank, turn around and look at our footsteps. Do you see yours? They go from one place to another—to the bush, then the fence, here and there. Do you see mine? A straight line! And that, Frank, is how to get through this life. Keep your eyes focused on what you want to do, and you will get to where you are going!"

On that day, Wright was said to have made a crucial promise to himself that he would never let his goals sidetrack him from enjoying life to the fullest. He wanted to be the kind of person who took time to look at the bushes and the farm animals, and to smell the roses. While still on the journey, he did not want to miss the scenery.

I think that is one of the things Jesus meant when he said he came to give us abundant life. The "life" in the promise here is a gift Jesus really wants to give us. The life Jesus is talking about is not the gift of resurrected or eternal life, nor is he saying what some foolish religious leaders promise: follow Jesus and everything you do will flourish and prosper—a terrible falsehood found nowhere in the Bible. No, what Jesus is trying to do is to remind us that each moment of life is a precious treasure.

It is so easy to be burdened by daily responsibilities; we all have them. There are, and always will be, so many tasks that go into fulfilling our goals of health, security, or professional success. Why not consider committing to making certain that our goals will not sidetrack us from enjoying the life we have been given?

Where to start? Just a few suggestions: spend some time watching a movie with a friend, spouse, child; or better yet, spend a bit more time talking together. Stop a few times a day, take a deep breath, and look out your window. Pray a bit more. Listen a bit more. Read a bit more. Or perhaps just stop a bit more.

Here is a list of things that will always be waiting for you: bills, the yard, phone calls, e-mails, the mail, your mortgage company, landlords, insurance bills, and many more. I am not suggesting they be ignored. They have to be tended to, just not all the time.

Here are some things that may not always be around: your child's story from school today, a rose that has just opened, a meal with a friend at a new restaurant, the first glass of wine from a new bottle, the first morning cup of coffee, your spouse reaching out to hold your hand, your mother who called "just to talk," your father who wants to pitch the ball or watch the game. You could miss new insights from your scripture reading as you start your day, and the voice you might hear or direction you may receive if you spend just a few minutes in the morning, or before bed, in prayer. You get the picture.

Abundant life is a very good gift if we receive it. Let us follow Frank Lloyd Wright around a bit and we may see something we might have missed.

— *Another Step . . .* —

What would happen if you simply pushed aside the mail, turned off your phone and computer, and had just a bit more silence in the day ahead?

A Prayer

Almighty God, still now, my rapid pace. Ease
my racing heart, still my racing mind, stop my
racing feet. Give me eyes to see, ears to hear, and
fingers to touch the abundant life springing up
all around me. Help me to find joy in this gift
You have given me, and to take each moment
as a precious jewel from Your hand into mine.
Amen.

—RJL+

Reality Check

The heavens are telling the glory of God; and the firmament proclaims his handiwork. Day to day pours forth speech, and night to night declares knowledge. There is no speech, nor are there words; their voice is not heard; yet their voice goes out through all the earth, and their words to the end of the world.

—Psalm 19:1–4

One summer while I was on vacation and visiting a small parish that rests on the north Atlantic coastline of Maine, the priest there decided to hold worship outdoors. The chairs faced our Lord's Table with a background of rushing waves smashing into the rugged boulders and layers of prehistoric rocks jutting out below. The sky, gently pocked with wisps of fluffy clouds, was a particular blue that no painter's brush could match. Gulls dove for unseen fish, and black cormorants stood motionless, holding out their wings to embrace the brisk winds.

I participated in the worship by listening to the lessons and sermon, singing the songs, praying the prayers, and consuming the Lord's Supper. As I did, words from scripture popped into my head, "The heavens are telling the glory of God."

"The heavens tell"—no words, no movie or play, no art or music, but the heavens themselves speak of God's majesty, handiwork, presence, and being.

We all know the phrase "reality check." It is usually a metaphorical slap in the face: "Hey! Wake up and pay attention, this is important!" Sometimes it comes in the form of a bill stamped

"Overdue" or a mortgage statement that reads "Final Notice." Sometimes the reality check is a coach or teacher raising their voice, calling our name, and saying, "Listen up!" Sometimes it is the doctor who comes in tapping the clipboard and says, "We have to talk," or the spouse who flips off the television and says, "You are not listening." A reality check usually gets us back on the track we are supposed to be traveling and off of which we have stumbled.

Nature has a number of reality checks, too: the chameleon that takes time to sun itself on a rock; the pup that delights in playing fetch; the mother hen embracing chicks under her wings; the oak tree with deep roots that last for centuries; the pecan tree with its shallow roots that topples when the ground is too wet; the anemone and clown fish, or shark and remora, that live with one another though completely different; the lioness who feasts with abandon, or the hyena that laughs with its mates; the sparks in a friend's eyes; the unclothed skin of a loved one with smooth and rolling landscapes of textures and shades; the stars that burn without apology, and the rising and setting sun—all which remind us of their constant presence.

It would be easy to ignore the reality check nature offers us. There is so much stuff that we humans make to tell our story. But that story is just a kind of chapter when held up against the stage of God's majestic epic. Don't see Him? Look up, look around, just look.

— *Another Step . . .* —

Sometime today, God will likely surprise you with some lesson from the world He has created, if you just take time to look. Open your eyes. See if you can agree that the heavens are sending a little reality check that reminds you of the Glory of God.

A Prayer

I praised the earth, in beauty seen
With garlands gay of various green;
I praised the sea, whose ample field
Shone glorious as a silver shield;
And earth and ocean seemed to say
"Our beauties are but for a day!"

I praised the sun, whose chariot rolled
On wheels of amber and of gold;
I praised the moon, whose softer eye
Gleamed sweetly through the summer sky,
And moon and sun in answer said,
"Our days of light are numbered!"

O God! O good beyond compare!
If thus thy meaner works are fair;
If thus thy bounties gild the span
Of ruined earth and sinful man;
How glorious must the mansion be
Where thy redeemed shall dwell with thee!

—Reginald Heber, d. 1826
A Bishop of Calcutta[22]

---

22 Counsell, *2000 Years of Prayer*, 355.

Serving Marvelously

For we are what he has made us, created in Christ Jesus for good works, which God prepared before-hand to be our way of life.

—Ephesians 2:10

"A domino factum est illud, et est mirabile in oculis meis!" When news reached Elizabeth that she would be the new reigning monarch of England upon the death of her sister Mary, these were the words she was heard to say.

Translation: "This is the doing of the Lord and it is marvelous in our eyes."[23]

In the life story of Queen Elizabeth I, one of the things that seems evident all of her life is that she was prepared for her role as one of the most significant and influential monarchs in the history of the United Kingdom. Her gifts and the needs of her country were a perfect fit for the season of her leadership.

If you are an adult much beyond the age of twenty-five, then you probably have witnessed a funeral for a well-known political figure, be it a president or prime minister, senator, governor, civic or religious leader. When death occurs, mourning and thanksgiving begin, and those of good character seem to be able to rise to the occasion and praise the changes such a leader has made throughout their work in the world.

One of the underlying principles of Christianity is that we were put on this earth to do something. But Christianity also teaches us

---

23 Psalm 118:23.

that you do not have to be the Queen of England, a governor, a
bank president, or a celebrity to do something important.

Christianity says that when we respond to work that God asks
us to do: living out our calling. There are certainly some big jobs
in the world's eyes, but whatever we are called to do with our
lives, if we are living into your calling it is big in God's eyes.
That goes for stay-at-home moms and dads, for garbage collectors, pool cleaners, and, yes, for CEOs, rock stars, and pastors.
This is why Paul writes the words above to the Christians scattered throughout the region of Ephesus. Perhaps a modern translation of Paul's words might be, "Don't forget—you were created
by God for a purpose: to do good things, to carry out good work;
that's the way we are supposed to live."

From time to time it is good to revisit our calling. "Why
am I doing what I am doing? Am I living into my call as fully
as I could? What needs to be added in, cut out, or changed?"
Frederick Buechner offers some good words:

> Vocation . . . It comes from the Latin "vocare," to call,
> and means the work a man is called to do by God.
> There are different kinds of voices calling you to all
> different kinds of work, and the problem is to find out
> which is the voice of God rather than of Society, or the
> Superego, or Self-Interest. By and large a good rule for
> finding out is this. The kind of work God usually calls
> you to is the kind of work (a) that you need most to
> do and (b) that the world most needs to have done. If
> you really get a kick out of your work, you've presum-
> ably met (a), but if your work is writing TV deodorant
> commercials, the chances are you've missed require-
> ment (b). On the other hand, if your work is being
> a doctor in a leper colony, you have probably met
> requirement (b), but if most of the time you're bored
> or depressed by it, the chances are you have not only
> bypassed (a) but probably aren't helping your patients
> much either. Neither the hair shirt nor the soft berth

will do. The place God calls you to is the place where your deep gladness and the world's hunger meet.[24]

Perhaps it is time to spend a few ticks of the clock to reflect on what you are doing with your life. Can you say of your vocation *"A domino factum est illud, et est mirabile in oculis meis"*? If not, begin to pray about what would be "marvelous in his eyes," and yours. But if you have found your calling, then do not forget to give thanks for the marvelous gift of vocation—a calling that is only yours and a need in the world that can only be met by you.

— *Another Step . . .* —

Are you living into your vocation? Why did you choose to "do" what you are doing? Is it a match between your gifts and the world's needs? Is it time for a change or time simply to pause and give thanks?

A Prayer

O send thy light and thy truth, that we may live always near to thee, our God. Let us feel thy love, that we may be as it were already in heaven, that we may do all our work as the angels do theirs. Let us be ready for every work, be ready to go out or come in, to stay or to depart, just as thou shalt appoint. Lord, let us have no will of our own, or consider our true happiness as depending in the slightest degree on anything that can befall us outwardly, but as consisting altogether in conformity to thy will; through Jesus Christ our Lord. *Amen.*

—Henry Martyn, d. 1812

A missionary and priest[25]

24 Buechner, *Wishful Thinking*, 95.
25 Counsell, *2000 Years of Prayer*, 354.

The One Who's Got Your Back

"The Lord is my rock, my fortress, and my deliverer, my God, my rock, in whom I take refuge, my shield and the horn of my salvation, my stronghold and my refuge, my savior; you save me from violence. I call upon the Lord, who is worthy to be praised, and I am saved from my enemies."

—2 Samuel 22:2–4

Protection. The word alone brings both a sense of comfort and perhaps heightened anxiety. We all want protection, and the thought of not having it creates angst, as if there is no covering, no footing, no "refuge," as David says above.

I have been fortunate to meet and spend time with three former presidents. The first time I had to go through not hours, but days of screening and background checks. In subsequent meetings, whether while attending a meeting or riding in a motorcade, the security was on every side. Windows were bulletproof; Secret Service agents were ubiquitous. Firearms were often hidden, but at times out in the open. There is no question that such security, particularly in today's world, is necessary. No question that there are those who, in the words well known to most teens, "had the President's back." And to be honest, on those occasions I, too, was grateful for the added security—the refuge.

But few of us have that kind of protection. And even if we did, it does not protect from everything, like tragedy and disease. Even still, I would bet most of us would like it.

My college roommate introduced me to a spray-on coating that when applied to the dashboard, leather or vinyl seating, the steering wheel, and even auto tires, made the surface look almost new in an instant. This spray-on "armor" gave the impression that the material underneath was protected from the external elements. But, of course, within a few days the coating wore thin and the dinks showed up again.

Who has got your back? Is there a kind of armor coating you can find to protect you from the slings and arrows of this world? A full bank account can provide job security, a large home, the right car, perhaps even the right reputation or friends. While some of these may enhance our lives, ultimately they do not provide a real refuge.

When David wrote the words here, he was besieged not only by real enemies, but also with a multitude of personal problems. He did not turn to armor, weapons, wealth, or the ancient equivalent to the Secret Service. He knew that when the going really got tough, God had his back.

Of course, we all take measures to protect ourselves from physical harm that could befall anyone—an alarm system, airport security, eating right, and wearing our seatbelts. But these are not refuges that can ultimately give us salvation.

When Jerusalem was so far from the place that God wanted that holy city to be, Jesus took pity on her and said, "How often have I desired to gather your children together as a hen gathers her brood under her wings" (Luke 13:34). It was Jesus's way of saying he wanted to protect the people he loved. He wanted them to know he had their backs. He has ours too.

It is not that God was not looking out for David; he was. It was not that Jesus was not looking out for Jerusalem; he was. The Secret Service is always looking out for the President, whether he is awake or asleep, whether he is attentive to the protection or not; they are always there.

David's prayer was not so much a plea as it was a personal reminder to be in touch with the one who had his back and has ours.

—— *Another Step . . .* ——
When do you find yourself most fearful? What comfort is there for you in knowing that God "has your back"?

A Prayer
May Jesus go before us to guide us;
Be beneath us to secure us;
Be behind us to protect us;
Be above us to watch over us;
And be beside us to befriend and bless us;
All the days of our life. *Amen.*

—The Reverend Dr. John Claypool, d. 2005

Who Is on Your Throne?

". . . he is Lord of lords and King of kings, and those with Him are called and chosen and faithful."

—Revelation 17:14

One of the astounding claims about Jesus of Nazareth was that when it came to authority, the buck stopped with him. The passage above is a piece of the apocalyptic visions of the end of time when evil will finally be vanquished. During Jesus's life, calling Him "king" was cause for praise by some and condemnation by others.[26]

Christians today often refer to Jesus as their king. Such kingship is probably not easily lived out in our day-to-day lives; many things vie for the throne of our hearts. Calling Jesus king gives us the opportunity to stop and consider who or what really is the center of our lives—who is boss, so to speak. In the United States it is difficult for us to fully understand what it would mean to have a monarch, as they do in the United Kingdom and other parts of the world. In a worldly sense, a monarch is to be followed and obeyed without reservation or question; the assumption is the monarch knows what is best for the land. We know the frailty of humanity has produced no perfect monarchs. But one did walk the earth.

Jesus speaks much of his kingdom and says it is "not of this world."[27] Jesus was constantly giving us glimpses into that realm through his teachings, actions, healings, as well as his death, resurrection, and ascension. Following Jesus as the monarch of our

---

26 Luke 19:38; Matthew 27:11.
27 John 18:33–37.

lives has tremendous implications. When we take a stand for Jesus, we reveal our allegiance to the kingdom to which we belong. Let me give you a good example.

A few years back, it was reported that a British Airways ticket agent was told by a supervisor to take off the small cross she was wearing. She decided to take voluntary leave rather than remove the cross. The story created a furor once it hit the news cycle. Everyone from political action committees to the Archbishop of York had an opinion. A friend of mine who is an editor and writer, David Kalvelage, reflected on this little cultural battle. After the dust settled, he wrote:

> A cross is the most identifiable symbol of being a Christian . . . Christians who wear a cross show others that they embrace the Christian way of life. The cross is also a sign of Christ's suffering and his eternal victory over death. Those who wear it should be willing to take up their cross and follow him. The woman who refused to remove it witnessed to her faith more effectively than most of us will ever do.[28]

Not everyone who wears a cross does so to express allegiance to Christ or a life of Christian discipleship, but the story reminds us that every day, most of us have not one chance, but multiple opportunities to declare our allegiance to our king; whether that moment is in public or in the private corners of our lives, how we respond will tell us who calls the shots.

Before you make your choice, remember we Christians believe that our creation, redemption, and purpose spring to life from Christ. The same One who created you also knows the secrets of joy and the perfect way to live your life. Why then would any of us ever choose any other king but Christ?

---

28 David Kalvelage, *The Living Church* (November 19, 2006), 11.

— *Another Step . . .* —

See your heart as a throne. Who or what is sitting on that throne as your king?

A Prayer

O Lord; O King, resplendent on the citadel of heaven,
All hail continually;
And of your clemency upon your people still have mercy.
Lord, whom the hosts of cherubim in songs and hymns
With praise continually proclaim, upon us eternally have mercy.
The armies aloft, O Lord, sing high praise to you;
Those to whom the seraphim reply, "have mercy."
O Christ, enthroned as king above,
Whom the nine orders of angels in their beauty
    Praise without ceasing,
Upon us, your servants, ever have mercy.
O Christ, hymned by your one and only church
    Throughout the world,
To whom the sun, and moon, and stars, the land and sea,
Ever do service, have mercy.
O Christ, those holy ones, the heirs of the eternal country,
One and all with utter joy proclaim you in a most worthy strain;
Have mercy upon us.
O Lord, O gentle son of Mary free;
O King of kings, blessed redeemer;
Upon those who have been ransomed from the power of death,
By your own blood ever have mercy.
O noblest unbegotten Son, having no beginning,
Yet without effort (in the weakness of God) excelling all things,
Upon this your people in your pity, Lord have mercy.
O sun of righteousness, in all unclouded glory,
    supreme dispenser of justice,

in that great day when you strictly judge all nations,
we earnestly beseech you, upon this your people,
who here stand before your presence,
in your pity, Lord, then have mercy on us.

—Dunstan, d. 988
Archbishop of Canterbury[29]

29 Counsell, *2000 Years of Prayer*, 92.

One Worth Worshipping

Then God spoke all these words: I am the Lord your God, who brought you out of the land of Egypt, out of the house of slavery; you shall have no other gods before me.

—Exodus 20:1–3

Season after season, *American Idol* has proven to be arguably one of the most successful entertainment franchises in world history. In one recent season over fifty million votes were cast for the winner. One Associated Press poll reported that thirty-five percent of Americans believed votes on Idol mattered as much as those cast in a U.S. Presidential election.

An idol, in the sense of a popular figure, is defined as "a person or thing that is greatly admired, loved, or revered." In spiritual terms, idolatry can be defined as the divine worship given to anyone or anything other than the true God, and worshipping anything other than God is wrong—flat-out, plain old, no-bones-about-it wrong.

The first four of the Ten Commandments in some way point to the sin of idolatry. The first in a list usually denotes priority, and the first commandment is no exception when God says through Moses, "You shall have no other gods."

In the last meditation, we looked a bit at paying tribute to the Divine as a king. Calling one king or queen usually has to do with matters of authority. Words like obedience, rule, perhaps even treason come to mind. A king may win our hearts, but not always. But worshipping has more to do with heart: affection, devotion, or homage. What is the problem with paying a little homage elsewhere?

Well, God said "No other gods" for a good reason. God knew we humans often run after the wrong thing to feed the hunger of our hearts and quench the thirsts of our souls. The problem is that nothing but God will ever be enough. I speak from personal experience here; I have tried other things. From time to time, I find those idols slipping into that place of devotion in my heart.

All kinds of things can be gods; most of them have a rather addictive quality. Success can be a god. Pleasure can be a god. A hobby can be a god. Family can be a god, which is why, sometimes, you see a family break apart when one or more members spin out of control. Food, rest, drink, sex, books, and chocolate—the list goes on. Do you remember the story of the Mt. Everest climbers who walked past David Sharp, a man who had collapsed from a lack of oxygen? Unwilling to stall their own ascent, dozens of people ignored him, and he died a few hours later. Sir Edmund Hillary, who first climbed the summit in 1953, said it was horrifying that climbers would leave a dying man.

Now a bit of clarification. There is nothing intrinsically wrong with, let us say, money. For instance, a common misquote of the Bible is, "Money is the root of all evil," when the actual quote is, "The love of money is a root of all kinds of evil" (1 Timothy 6:10). There is nothing sinful, at ground zero, with watching or enjoying American Idol, playing golf, hunting, cross stitching, or loving your children. The problem comes when that devotion, love, and commitment, in any sense, replace what is owed to the One who created, redeemed, saved, and sustains us.

So as we consider who is on the throne of our hearts, perhaps we can also consider who or what has the affection of our hearts so much so that we are willing to worship the object of our affection. "What" may need to be chucked out of the way of that "who." Our Lord visited this planet earth for all kinds of reasons, one of which was to convict us of those things that are not right in our bodies, souls, hearts, and strength. Perhaps that is why Jesus said the greatest commandment was, in fact, to love God with those four aspects of our beings.[30] But another reason Jesus came was to create in us clean hearts and to renew our own spirits, which means that we always have the chance to begin again, if we are willing to turn from whatever our favorite idol is and make the God of all creation the primary object of our affection.[31]

Do not let your own "idol worship" be the death of you; also do not slip into despair. The good news is that when we invite Jesus in to mend us, our health begins to be restored and it will carry us through this life to the next. The One that does that for us is One worth worshipping.

— *Another Step . . .* —

What idols pull the devotion of your heart away from worshipping God? Make a list and then call on God to help you release anything that stands in the way of your pure devotion to him.

A Prayer

Father, as we now prepare to share in the activity
of worship, cleanse our hearts and minds, fill us
with your Holy Spirit, and open our lips to show
forth your praise; for the sake of Jesus Christ our
Lord. *Amen.*[32]

---

30 Mark 12:30.
31 Psalm 51:10.
32 Frank Coloquhoun, *Contemporary Parish Prayers* (London: Hodder & Stoughton Religious, 2005).

Help!

"All things are lawful for me," but not all things are beneficial. "All things are lawful for me," but I will not be dominated by anything.

—1 Corinthians 6:12

On one of my days off, my family and I spent a bit of time exploring the city in which I now live. The greater Houston area offers no shortage of things to do, so it was hard to know where to begin. Needless to say, a trip to the Galleria was early on the agenda.

The biggest draw for our youngest was the ice skating rink. I, somewhat reluctantly, joined him on the ice. I kept thinking how I would explain an injury to my parishioners. It had been years since I had given skating a whirl, but after a while I got used to the ice. While no tricks were involved, there were no spills either. How humbling to see six-year-olds speed and spin around me.

At one point, however, I got going a bit faster than expected and realized I was not real clear on the stopping bit. Heading full tilt toward a curve, I, with a great deal of embarrassment, slammed into the wall surprising a young mom who was keeping an eye on her kids from the sidelines. I smiled, swallowed my pride, apologized for giving her a little jolt and said, "I've got the going part down, it's the stopping that I haven't got yet."

Believe it or not, my mind quickly turned to the words that the apostle Paul used when writing to the church in Corinth: not all things are beneficial. In these last few meditations, we have been wrestling with improper priorities (kingship, idolatry). It could be said that a real issue related to both keeping the proper king on the throne and steering clear of idols is excess. The idea is that there can be "too much of a good thing."

Too often, perhaps, we focus on the bad in the world around us. Paul's point was a reminder that God's real desire is for us to enjoy life. When things go awry it is usually because we, out of ignorance, selfishness, or perhaps downright rottenness, have taken something good and turned it in a way God did not intend. I think that's why the verse came to mind when I slammed into the wall at the Polar Ice Rink: most of us have the *going* part down, it is the *stopping* part that is often hard to manage. But when we forget that, we also tend to forget there are always messy and painful consequences to our wrongful actions. I noticed the small print on my ice skating ticket: ". . . by accepting this ticket patron hereby accepts any and all inherent risk associated with ice sports . . . ." Much in life could bear a similar warning label.

God made food, and a good meal is wonderful, but the intent was not gluttony. God made the pieces of a good wine, but not with the hope of drunkenness. Sexual intimacy was one of God's most wonderful gifts to humankind, not to be lived out indiscriminately or promiscuously, but within that context of marriage and fidelity. Having our basic needs met is a good thing. Even luxury can be a good thing, but kept "unchecked" it can quickly spin out of control and all kinds of ugly fruits begin to pop out—excess, selfish ambition, materialism.

The problem with many of the good things gone bad is we know how to do the going, but not so much the *stopping.* How do we remedy the problem? Reflection at the end of each day, spiritual direction from your clergy, the support of Christian fellowship, the gift of worship, the wealth of knowledge available through the Holy Scriptures and the way our Lord works in and through all of these things, and many more.

One chief avenue is prayer. When we see that wall approaching quickly, when we feel like we've begun to breach the God-given levee, we reach out with heart and voice in prayer. *"Help!"* It is a good starting place at getting a handle not just on the *going,* but the *stopping* as well.

— *Another Step . . .* —

Spend some time reflecting on an area of your life in which
something may be lawful, but not beneficial. In short, where
is the excess that needs to be controlled?

A Prayer

Almighty God, Who alone can bring order to the
unruly wills and passions of sinful humanity: Give
your people grace so to love what you command and
to desire what you promise, that, among the many
changes of this world, our hearts may surely there be
fixed where true joys are to be found; through Jesus
Christ our Lord. *Amen*.[33]

---

33 Andrew Burnham, comp. *A Pocket Manual of Anglo-Catholic Devotion* (New York:
Canterbury, 2003), 197.

Ouch

Then Job answered the Lord: "I know that you can do all things, and that no purpose of yours can be thwarted. 'Who is this that hides counsel without knowledge?' Therefore I have uttered what I did not understand, things too wonderful for me, which I did not know. 'Hear, and I will speak; I will question you, and you declare to me.' I had heard of you by the hearing of the ear, but now my eye sees you; therefore I despise myself, and repent in dust and ashes."

—Job 42:1–6

"The patience of Job" is probably something that you have either said or have heard said at some time during your life. But if you know the rather long and depressing story of Job, you know that Job did not have patience; it ran out. As we say in my part of the country, when he had reached the rope's end, he pitched a fit. He basically raised his hand and said, "Hey, I don't get it. I'm a pretty good guy. I thought we had some kind of deal. I just don't understand what's up with all this suffering."

Suffering and pain (short or long term) are no fun. They hurt. Physical pain usually can be numbed, but not so for other kinds of pain—emotional, mental, even spiritual. Whether we walk with God or not, it may be that out of our pain, we take time to shake our fist to the sky and ask, "Why?"

It may seem simple, and perhaps not the best balm for an ailing wound, to hear sometimes the answer is just beyond our grasp. Sometimes when we ask God to stop the suffering, God says "No," sometimes "Wait," and sometimes "Trust me." Sometimes we actually grow through pain and suffering. I do not think God is a sadist, but I do think often there is more to suffering than meets the eye.

Storyteller Bruce Waltke said that as a boy at his grandparents' country home, he was walking in the forest and he came upon a rare sight: a small chrysalis spinning around, about to break open and release a new butterfly. Part of one wing broke through right at his eye level. He was moved by how hard the butterfly struggled to emerge from the cocoon.

Waltke thought, "I will just give him a little help." He reached down, ever so carefully and cut the top of the cocoon off with the hope of giving the butterfly a little relief in its journey toward growth. The butterfly came out quickly, but was still very damp. It stood for a while on the edge of the cocoon and then dropped to the floor and died. He said he learned something very important that day. Sometimes we need the struggle of emergence to survive.

Sometimes in the midst of pain or suffering we do not see what the end result may be. There is an old fable about a little piece of wood who was complaining because its owner was whittling away at it, cutting it, and filling it with holes. The one who was cutting so remorselessly paid no attention to the complaining. He was making a flute out of that piece of wood. Finally he said to the complaining stick, "Little piece of wood, without these holes and all this cutting, you would be a black stick forever—just a useless piece of ebony. What I am doing now may make you think I am destroying you, but instead, I will change you into a flute, and your sweet music will charm the souls of others and comfort many a sorrowing heart. My cutting is the making of you, for only thus can you be a blessing to the world."[34]

After Job pitched his fit, God responded with these words, "Who is this that darkens counsel by words without knowledge? Gird up your loins like a man. I will question you . . ." (Job 38:2–3). I would not want to have been on the other end of God's response.

Job responded, "Oh, you created the universe; you created me;

---

34 This quote was taken from personal notes kept throughout the author's ministry.

you have a much better view of things from where you sit. If it's okay, I'll just take all that back."

I do not mean to make light of suffering. Some of you reading this have suffered, and perhaps are suffering terrible things. I have as well. In the midst of some of those things, I could never have known how God might have redeemed them. But in most cases, he did. God still does.

⸺ *Another Step . . .* ⸺

Can you think of a time when God actually worked in your suffering? If you are suffering now, can you see God's hand at work? If not, then seek it out. If you cannot seek it out, just offer it up to Him in prayer.

A Prayer

O Lord God, our heavenly Father, regard, we pray, with Thy divine pity the pains of all Thy children; and grant that the Passion of our Lord and His infinite love may make fruitful for good the tribulations of the innocent, the suffering of the sick, and the sorrows of the bereaved; through Him who suffered in our flesh and died for our sake, the same thy Son Jesus Christ our Lord. *Amen.*

—A prayer that was published and
encouraged for use during World War I[35]

---

35 Counsell, *2000 Years of Prayer,* 468.

Yea, Thou Art with Me

The Lord is my shepherd, I shall not want. He makes me lie down in green pastures; he leads me beside still waters; he restores my soul. He leads me in right paths for his name's sake. Even though I walk through the darkest valley, I fear no evil; for you are with me . . . .

—Psalm 23:1–4

I spent the better part of today preparing for a memorial service for a member of my parish. A family member asked, as hundreds before her have, that we read Psalm 23—a portion of which is above. Perhaps the most moving line in the psalm for those who struggle with dark valleys is that last bit, maybe better known in the traditional King James Version: "Yea though I walk through the valley of the shadow of death . . . Thou art with me . . . ."

Why are those words so comforting? In the last meditation we looked at what we can learn from suffering, but allow me to go farther. If we "get" the lesson of suffering, can we not just "get" to the end of the valley of the shadow of death? In the last meditation, I said that sometimes God's answer to us is, "Trust me. I know what I am doing." That really is hard, is it not? We would all like a god we can control. We would probably much prefer a god who is more like the ancient genie in the lamp.

I really like the story of Aladdin and his magic lamp. Disney did an rather good animated version a few years ago. The genie was funny, the bad guy lost, and Aladdin learned the value of being himself. But, as priest and writer Barbara Brown Taylor points out, there is another insight that is hard for a preacher to miss: a genie is much more appealing than God. With a genie you know you have three wishes that you can redeem whenever you like. If the genie gets on your nerves in the meantime, you can make him go back into his lamp and play solitaire until you need him again. *Your* will is his command; if you are like me on wish number three, you just wish for three more wishes.

The difference between God and a genie is clear. God is not in the business of granting wishes. God is in the business of bringing sight to the blind, wholeness to the broken, and new life to the dead.[36] While we are not promised that we do not have to walk through the valley of the shadow of death, we are promised that when we do, if we are willing to receive it, God will take our hand and travel alongside us.

There is a wonderful old prayer that says, "I said to the man who stood at the gate: 'Give me a light that I may tread safely into the unknown.' And he replied: 'Go out into the darkness and put your hand into the hand of God. That shall be to you better than light and safer than a known way.'"[37] Few people I have met have understood this better than a young friend of mind named Emily.

Emily was a Latin major at the University of the South where I served as a chaplain some years ago. Shortly after her birth, Emily contracted rheumatic fever and as a result, rheumatoid arthritis. When this illness strikes, it is merciless and often crippling for life. Emily is just under five feet tall, unable to bend her legs. She used to ride a small cart around campus and had to depend on fellow classmates to carry her up stairs—an experience she and I shared on more than one occasion.

The growth of her arms and fingers was stunted, so holding eating utensils and carrying a meal tray were daily challenges. Over the years of her adolescence, Emily had an average of two operations every twelve months; her body carried the scars of

36 Barbara Brown Taylor, *Gospel Medicine* (Boston: Cowley Publications, 1995), 109–110.
37 Batchelor, *The Doubleday Prayer Collection*, 146.

hopeful treatments. Emily is one of the most delightful people I have ever met. She never seemed embarrassed, and I have never heard her complain. I long wondered the secret of her contentment.

One evening, I asked her to speak about her life to the college community. She walked her hearers through what most would describe as a lifetime of horrors: surgery after surgery, one try after another to establish some sort of normalcy. The words that will ring in my ears for as long as I have memory were those she used as she closed: "If I had my life to live over again, I wouldn't change a thing. This affliction has demanded that I walk with God daily, depend on him constantly, for my very survival. I know he loves me as I am and I know he is the source of real life."

This young Christian had every reason to give up on God and on life, but her commitment to Christ brought as much healing to her as if her crippled limbs were restored to wholeness. Emily did not let suffering get the best of her, and she was healed not in body, but in soul. And for her, that was all that mattered. What I saw was not the desperate illness, but the power of God being revealed in her life.

When it seems like you are in that valley of the shadow of death, grab hold of God and say, "Yea, thou art with me."

— *Another Step . . .* —

Are you traveling through the valley of the shadow of death right now? Are you holding God's hand? Are you letting God hold yours? If not, perhaps start now.

A Prayer

Lord, make possible for me by grace what is impossible to me by nature. You know that I am not able to endure very much, and that I am downcast by the slightest difficulty. Grant that for Your sake I may come to love and desire any hardship that puts me to the test, for salvation is brought to my soul when I undergo suffering and trouble for you.

—Thomas à Kempis, d. 1471[38]

---

38 Batchelor, *The Doubleday Prayer Collection*, 165.

Trusting the Engineer

Listen to advice and accept instruction, that you may gain wisdom for the future. The human mind may devise many plans, but it is the purpose of the Lord that will be established.

—Proverbs 19:20–21

I got a call, which is not uncommon in my vocation, that a member of my parish had an unexpected setback in recovery from a medical procedure. It was not critical or life-threatening. She had hoped to move along quicker and get back to work and play, but those plans changed because of an unexpected setback—frankly, an unwelcome change of plans.

A good friend told me something that I had never spent much time thinking about. She said, "Anger is usually the result of disappointment in unmet expectations." Though anger has many sources, the more I have thought her words, the more I figure she is right. When I get crossed up with someone, it is usually because they disappointed me. It was not what I had planned.

We all have plans for our marriages, friendships, relationships, work, health, or what we hope to accomplish. Then things upset our expectations and plans. When things do not go the way we planned, we end up shocked or surprised, disappointed or grief-stricken, or maybe we are just downright angry. What do we do with those kinds of disappointments? There are lots of pithy phrases that may get us through a bad day—"When life hands you lemons, make lemonade"—but they will not carry us through the anger or disappointment.

The book of Proverbs is a fascinating collection of pithy sayings: thirty-one chapters of insight and wisdom attributed to Solomon. The proverb that starts this meditation instructs us to make way for learning by listening. Interestingly, it is coupled with a kind of reflection on making plans. It says the human heart may make all kinds of plans but, in the end, what really matters is trying to live into God's guidance. Trusting that plans will come out the way we hope often leads to disappointment; trusting in God gives one the ability to move beyond the anger of unmet expectations. "Let go and let God," the saying goes. In other words, plans are nice, but God is better than any plan.

The apostle Paul, as you probably know, did not plan to follow Jesus, but his encounter with the risen Lord changed his plans.[39] He wanted to be one kind of religious leader; he ended up being another kind. He had planned on enjoying the fruits of his success, but wherever he went, trouble seemed to meet him, or at the very least was close behind. At life's end, he found himself in prison facing Roman executioners. He had a taste of imprisonment when he was under house arrest in Ephesus, and there he wrote one of his most remarkable letters, the power-packed letter to the Philippians. In it, it is clear that Paul had begun to reflect on how his life's plans went asunder. "I have learned to be content with whatever I have. I know what it is to have little, and I know what it is to have plenty. In any and all circumstances, I have learned the secret of being well-fed and of going hungry, of having plenty and of being in need." Then he ends by revealing his secret, "I can do all things through Him who strengthens me" (Philippians 4:11–13).

Paul's secret was that he knew being linked to God, through Christ and in the power of the Holy Spirit, gave him a deep sense of contentment. It was not blissful ignorance or naïve giddiness, but a kind of inward assurance that God would get him through anything. When Paul wrote to the Church in Rome, "We know that all things work together for good for those who love God," he

---

39 Acts 9.

did not mean that God fixed everything; he meant that God could in any kind of circumstance. My guess is plenty of folks face the crisis of unexpected setbacks daily. And many could share stories of how God was and is working in their midst, from something as monumental as finding the right physician at the right time to something as miniscule as having a spouse hold their hand as they wait for the doctor to come in with an update.

And in your own crisis? God is there. Look around. Be patient. Do not let anger get hold of you. Instead, hold on to God, because God is surely holding onto you. Hold on to those who come your way; you will see them if you look hard enough. Holding on to both helps us get through those "perfect moments" that did not turn out so perfect. In the end, God will turn it into its own kind of resurrection, if we just let him.

Let me offer a pithy phrase from one of my heroes, Corrie Ten Boom, who survived the Ravensbruck concentration camp. My guess is during those dark days, her plans were not going quite like she hoped. She said, "When a train goes through a tunnel and it gets dark, you don't throw away your ticket and jump off. You sit still and trust the engineer."[40] May I suggest we keep trusting "the engineer" even when things do not quite turn out like we planned? In time, God will get us where we need to be.

— *Another Step . . .* —

In what circumstance do you find discontentment right now? When have your plans not turned out as you had hoped? Looking more closely into the circumstance or the changed plan, do you see God's hand? Do you see God's plan? Is His better than yours?

---

40 This quote was taken from personal notes kept throughout the author's ministry.

A Prayer

Teach me, O God, so to use all the circumstances of my life
Today that they may bring forth in me the fruits of holiness
Rather than the fruits of sin.
Let me use disappointments as material for patience:
Let me use success as material for thankfulness:
Let me use suspense as material for perseverance:
Let me use danger as material for courage:
Let me use reproach as material for longsuffering:
Let me use praise as material for humility:
Let me use pleasure as material for temperance:
Let me use pains as material for endurance.
Amen.

—John Baillie, d. 1960[41]

---

41 John Baillie, *A Diary of Private Prayer* (New York: Fireside, 1996), 101.

Law and Grace

For by grace you have been saved through faith, and this is not your own doing; it is the gift of God—not the result of works, so that no one may boast. For we are what he has made us, created in Christ Jesus for good works, which God prepared beforehand to be our way of life.

—Ephesians 2:8–10

After my first year of college, I went scuba diving with three friends off the Gulf Coast of Florida. Due to a series of foolish mistakes, I not only ran out of air at sixty feet below the surface, but when I reached the top with my buddy—who saved my life— we found we were also separated from our boat.

Being a young, robust, and foolish man, I said to my friend, "Let's just dump the tanks and swim to shore." Of course, I was ignoring the challenges of the currents, the distance, the sharks, and the reality of my own weakness. My friend chose the better option of staying afloat and yelling for help. A wave carried us high enough for another fishing boat to see the tip of my friend's spear gun waving back and forth in the air.

It was not until I was pulled into the boat that I realized I had been rescued, and that I played absolutely no role in the rescue other than to receive it. It was, and continues to be for me, a real image of what our faith calls *grace*. When the apostle Paul writes, "by grace you have been saved," he means we can do *absolutely nothing* to contribute to our salvation.

Earlier on in this little set of meditations, I wrote of the Cross where those who flee for forgiveness and redemption receive it—the burned-over place. As we have unpacked other aspects of Christianity in these last several meditations, it is prudent to drop a reminder that much, if not all, of Christianity and its benefits are gifts.

We humans do not like to hear that we get something we have not earned. We tend to have rather inflated views of ourselves and prefer to win our way to the trophy, promotion, or salary boost. It does not work that way with God's grace. We do not win God's approval by our moral purity, good deeds of Christian charity, theological acumen, or religious devotion. Grace says to each of these efforts on our behalf, "Sorry, it is by grace you are saved, not by you that you are saved."

Certainly our morality, theology, good deeds, and religious devotion are part of our life in Christ, but such actions grow out of our love for Christ, not as an attempt to win him over. In much the same way, certain expressions of marriage (mutual support, intimacy, the building of a family) or friendship (communication, companionship) are not what make those relationships work. It is love that serves as the greatest cord that binds; the rest are cords that grow out from it. If my friendships or marriage depended on my fulfilling my duties, I would fail miserably and live under the constant burden of "Am I doing it right?"

It is a good thing that my salvation does not depend on me. If I were to pile up the good and bad alongside one another, I think the scales would tip more toward the manure in the garden than the flowers I have grown. That is just the way it is. I have to turn the whole garden over to "The Gardener." The only part we play is to receive. Grace is God's work; faith is how we receive God's work. To suggest otherwise is an insult to the death of Christ—and I do not think that is too hard of a word.

In his book, *The Grace of God*, William MacDonald says:

> To seek to earn, merit, or purchase salvation is to insult the Giver. Imagine yourself invited to a banquet in the White House by the President of the United States. You are seated at a table that is filled with the choicest

foods. Every effort is made to give you a most enjoyable evening. At the end of a lovely visit, the President stands at the front door to bid you good-bye.

What do you do? As you leave, do you press a dime into his hand and say "Thank you very much for your kindness. I have enjoyed the evening very much. I realize it has cost you a lot of money, and I want to help you pay for the meal."

Is that the proper response to his kindness? On the contrary it is a rude and insulting gesture. So it would be with God's grace.[42]

The real difference is between law and grace. Winning our way to God's favor via the law means I will never get there. If I had depended on myself alone to get me out of my diving mess, I would be as dead as the dodo bird. Grace says we already have God's favor and, when we receive that via faith, we are rescued and new life begins, as it was when I was rescued both by my diving buddy and the captain of our little boat. That is the gospel, plain and simple.

Kenneth Wuest once wrote a little verse that puts it this way:

"Do this and live!" the Law demands,
But gives me neither feet nor hands.
A better word God's grace does bring,
It bids me fly and gives me wings.[43]

Thank God for that. I think I will take grace over law any day. How about you?

42 William MacDonald, *The Grace of God* (Kansas City: ECS Ministries, 1960), pamphlet.
43 Kenneth Wuest, *Romans in the Greek New Testament*, Vol. 2 (Eerdmans, 1955), 378.

—— *Another Step* . . . ——

Think on some ways you might try and "earn" God's love. How does it change your view of things to know that God loves you already?

A Prayer

Amazing grace! How sweet the sound,
That saved a wretch like me!
I once was lost but now am found,
Was blind but now I see.

'Twas grace that taught my heart to fear,
and grace my fears relieved;
how precious did that grace appear
the hour I first believed.[44]

—John Newton, d. 1807

---

44 From the hymn, *Amazing Grace*, stanzas 1 and 2.

Be Holy

Beloved, while eagerly preparing to write to you about the salvation we share, I find it necessary to write and appeal to you to contend for the faith that was once for all entrusted to the saints. For certain intruders have stolen in among you, people who long ago were designated for this condemnation as ungodly, who pervert the grace of our God into licentiousness and deny our only Master and Lord, Jesus Christ.

—Jude 1:3–4

At one summer camp, I accidentally stepped dead onto a wooden splinter that went right into the ball of my foot. To this day, I can still hear my twelve-year-old voice, interrupted only by my hopping about, yelling, "Take it out! Take it out!" I received first aid from a sixteen-year-old counselor who pulled the small spear out with a pair of pliers and told me to wash my foot and get back to play time.

About ten days later, I stepped on that spot in just the right way and it sent a sharp pain all the way up into my leg. I pulled off my shoes and socks to find it was badly infected. I went to the camp nurse who promptly gave me a tongue depressor and told me to turn my head and hold on because she was out of Novocain and would have to dig out what was evidently the remaining part of the tiny javelin. She was successful; I still have the scar to prove it. Until I got all of the problem out, I had to keep dealing with the infection. Infection and a healthy body do not go hand in hand.

The book of Jude is only one chapter. Actually, it's a letter. We are not sure who wrote it. Some have thought perhaps Jesus's brother; others think it might be the "other Judas."[45] In any case, it was an early church leader who was fighting a growing problem in the early days of Christianity: the belief that somehow, because one had encountered the grace of Christ and were already "saved," they could behave as they wanted. If one is already "in" with God, what did it matter what they did with their body or mind?

This thinking was an outgrowth of the popular Gnostic movement. The budding religion embraced several Christian doctrines, but also held that the body (the literal, fleshy body) was so corrupt and evil that it could never possibly be good or holy. Suffice it to say, since Gnosticism shared some of the tenets of Christianity, some of the Gnostics slipped into the Christian community.

A religion that teaches that you can have your head in the clouds and your feet in the brothel was very attractive to many, but it did not square with Christ. So Jude answered the challenge clearly, "intruders . . . pervert the grace of God into licentiousness." In short, grace is not a free pass. As noted in the last meditation, grace is a gift all around, but it is a gift that should prompt a change in us—in our behavior, thinking, lifestyle, ethics, and morality.

An outgrowth of a relationship with God in Christ is a holy life. Peter, evidently battling Gnosticism as well, reached into the Hebrew scriptures to remind Christians scattered throughout the ancient civilized world that God was clear about this holiness business, "Instead, as he who called you is holy, be holy yourselves in all your conduct; for it is written, 'You shall be holy, for I am holy.'"[46]

Along the way, we have touched on some issues related to forgiveness. There is no question God forgives, and forgives aplenty. In the last meditation, I touched on some thinking around grace. But forgiveness and the grace from which it springs are not green lights to live as we please. Christians are called to more than that.

---

45 Luke 6:16; Acts 1:13.
46 1 Peter 1:16; Leviticus 11:45.

You cannot continue to live with part of the infection left in the body. If you do, in time the infection will fester and eventually consume. Part of that invitation of grace says, "Here it is: it is given not because you scored points with me [God], but because I love you and do not want you to live in the vicious cycle of sin and guilt. I forgive you, and as I do, out of my love, I hope your love for me will grow and effect a change so that what you want more and more is not the infection, but the antibiotic."

Jude and Peter were right to try and convince early Christians that loving God meant doing more than going to church and Bible study; it meant a changed life. It still does. Not a perfect life, but a life that seeks to be healed more than destroyed, filled more than emptied, strengthened more than weakened, and made whole more than being infected.

—   *Another Step . . .*   —

Where have you left some of the splinter in? Perhaps it is time to pull the rest out and hand it over to the grace of God.

A Prayer

Almighty God, unto whom all hearts are open,
all desires known, and from whom no secrets
are hid: Cleanse the thoughts of our hearts by
the inspiration of thy Holy Spirit, that we may
perfectly love thee, and worthily magnify thy
holy Name; through Christ our Lord.[47]

—From the Book of Common Prayer

47 Book of Common Prayer, 323.

Bearing Fruit

"You did not choose me but I chose you. And I appointed you to go and bear fruit, fruit that will last . . . ."

—John 15:16

I am not a big fan of going to the mall. Aside from the crowds and the general hullabaloo, I sometimes wince at the interaction between parents and children, wives and husbands, boyfriends and girlfriends. The wince comes when I hear a string of harsh words. I am not writing about the occasional discipline that may be necessary; and perhaps you would join me in confessing that I have lost my temper in a long shopping line at one time or another. No, I am talking about something much more severe.

Not too long ago I was walking in front of a mother who was inappropriately and harshly speaking to her young son, who was perhaps no more than seven; she put him down not once, but several times. Later, as I was leaving the mall, I heard another parent severely scolding his child. I looked at a young lady in one of the mall kiosks and said, "I bet you see some very difficult things."

She answered, "All the time."

As I have pointed out in these last few meditations, we are not called to be perfect, but we are called to live the law of love with our fellow humans. The scriptures tell us the fuel that allows to live out love is the Holy Spirit of God, given to us at that point when we come into relationship with our Lord Christ. Living the law of love can be a daily challenge—often difficult for all kinds of reasons. But we are told that if we walk with our Lord, in time it will begin to show up in all kinds of ways.

Perhaps that is why the apostle Paul uses the imagery of fruit to describe some of the "produce" of a Spirit-filled life: "The fruit of the Spirit is love, joy, peace, patience, kindness, goodness, faithfulness, gentleness, and self-control" (Galatians 5:22–23). That is a pretty good list, a kind of maintenance check for the condition of our souls. Unlike "spiritual gifts" (next meditation), which seem to be parceled out differently to different people, these "fruits" are to be exhibited in our Christian life day to day.

How do we do that? We look at our lives. Do we see "fruits" growing, popping out, not because of a Herculean effort, but naturally? If not, then we need to go to our knees in silence and begin to work out and wrestle with those areas of our lives not yet submitted to Christ. Sometimes the end result is a big change, a full-blown lifestyle conversion. Sometimes it is simply a decision to begin living in one way over another.

I had a colleague in ministry who told me that he had reached a point of frustration in living out the fruits of goodness in his own life. A particular set of circumstances seemed to say to him that living in a loving way with others made no difference. Early in his ministry, his frustration hit a peak on one particular day and he angrily stormed into the office of his priest. He said, and I quote, "I have spent 32 years being a nice person and where has it gotten me!?"

His priest replied, "Would you like to spend the rest of your life as an angry person?"

"No," my friend answered.

"Then choose nice!" his priest said. I am happy to tell you he did.

I am not perfect and cannot promise anyone with whom I share life that I will not have days when I am rather fruitless, but I know accepting the grace of Christ into our lives and the Spirit that comes with it does give us the power to, in Jesus's words, "bear fruit." Why not take the counsel of that wise old priest? Let us choose the fruits of the Spirit.

— *Another Step* . . . —

Take a look at the list of Paul's fruits. Where do you fall short? Which ones do you see popping out? So what will you choose?

A Prayer

O God, thou has commanded us to walk in the Spirit and not to fulfill the lusts of the flesh; make us perfect, we pray, in love, that we may conquer our natural selfishness and give ourselves to others. Fill our hearts with thy joy, and garrison them with thy peace; make us long-suffering and gentle, and thus subdue our hasty and angry tempers; give us faithfulness, meekness and self-control; that so crucifying the flesh with its affections and lusts, we may bring forth the fruit of the Spirit to thy praise and glory; through Jesus Christ our Lord. *Amen.*

—Henry Alford, d. 1871
Former Dean of Canterbury Cathedral[48]

---

48 Counsell, *2000 Years of Prayer*, 362–363.

Living Sacrifices

I appeal to you therefore, brothers and sisters, by the mercies of God, to present your bodies as a living sacrifice, holy and acceptable to God, which is your spiritual worship. . . . For as in one body we have many members, and not all the members have the same function, so we, who are many, are one body in Christ, and individually we are members one of another. We have gifts that differ according to the grace given to us: prophecy, in proportion to faith; ministry, in ministering; the teacher, in teaching; the exhorter, in exhortation; the giver, in generosity; the leader, in diligence; the compassionate, in cheerfulness.

—Romans 12:1, 4–8

In my wife's family, we really have an "Aunt Bea." I have been the beneficiary of her hospitality, like hundreds of others. By hospitality, I do not mean simply staying over for a good meal and a warm bed. I mean an open and generous house to which you are welcomed, made to feel special, where nothing is expected but your pleasure and joy in visiting, eating, and taking delight in being tended to by one who has an extraordinary gift of hospitality.

My wife and I enjoy having people over and—when all the plans are carefully made—we love opening our home. That is what one might call "regular hospitality." What flows out of the heart of Aunt Bea is an extraordinary, some might say supernatural, gift of hospitality. You can show up at Aunt Bea's almost any hour of any day and you will be welcomed with open arms. The same is not true of my home; you might be welcomed, or I might switch off the porch light depending on the time of the night.

In the New Testament, we find several places where the gifts of the Holy Spirit are described.[49] Now gifts, unlike fruits (as I described in the last meditation), are unique to a person. Spiritual fruits are a natural outgrowth of a relationship with Christ; gifts are given to people as God so chooses. In other words, one may have hospitality (like Aunt Bea) or one may have teaching. The extraordinary, particular gift exercised through Christians is called the "Gift of the Spirit." It is, in a very real sense, a kind of miracle—a glimpse into the Kingdom and power of God.

There are three important pieces we should take hold of around these gifts. First, they are gifts. So you can take pride in them if you choose, but if they were handed to you by the One who designed the gifts, picked you to receive them, and counts on you to use them, would it not be better to thank the Giver, point to the Giver, and use the gifts in ways that glorify the Giver?

Second, it is important to identify your gifts. For this, you may need to seek the counsel of your priest or pastor. You may need to pray and reflect on those things that seem to come natural to you, but not so natural to others. You may also need to be honest about gifts you do not have. If you do not have the gift of teaching, then why try? Better to use the gift you have been given than to try and pretend like you have one you do not.

Thirdly, use your gift. Paul implores the Christians in ancient Rome to present themselves as "living sacrifices." That means they should pour out their lives, using the gifts they have been given, to others and to God. If we fast-forward to today, Paul's plea tells us when it comes to our own spiritual gifts we should not hoard, hide, reject, resent, or ignore our gifts, but use them to God's glory and for the benefit of God's people, and perhaps even for those who do not seem to have much use for God. Perhaps, through you and your gifts, they will be drawn to God.

---

49 1 Corinthians 12; Isaiah 11:1–5; Ezekiel 11:19; Psalm 127:3; 1 Corinthians 7:7; Philippians 4:7; Hebrews 4:1, 9; James 1:5, 4:6.

Pastor and devotional writer Chuck Swindoll likes to tell of an encounter he had with one man's spiritual gift.

> My life has been crossed by men who have the gift of giving. Maybe yours has also. When I was at Dallas Seminary, God used a man in my life and in the lives of ten other fellows at the school. [He] chose to under-write our tuition. Absolutely unsolicited. Each time tuition came due, there was a check in the mail.
>
> I remember one time he came to Dallas and got all eleven of us together and said, "I want us to take a drive downtown." After a sandwich, he took us several blocks away to a men's store. Inside he suited us up in new suits, new sports coats, one fellow after another. He sat there and just beamed! He was happier than we were! He wasn't wealthy, but there was something inside of him (it's called a spiritual gift) that was not satisfied until there was an outlet for that gift.[50]

Once you have found it, what do you do? Respond, with all you are, to Paul's invitation, "I appeal to you therefore, brothers and sisters, by the mercies of God, to present your bodies as a living sacrifice."

——   *Another Step . . .*   ——

Review the list of spiritual gifts and see if you can discern your gift or gifts. If so, are you putting them to work? If not, why not?

---

50 Charles R. Swindoll, *The Tale of the Tardy Oxcart* (Nashville: Thomas Nelson, 1998), 533.

A Prayer

Almighty and eternal God, so draw our hearts to
thee, so guide our minds, so fill our imaginations,
so control our wills, that we may be wholly Thine,
utterly dedicated unto thee; and then use us, we pray
thee, as thou wilt, but always to thy glory and the
welfare of thy people, through our Lord and Savior,
Jesus Christ.

—William Temple, d. 1944
Archbishop of Canterbury[51]

51 Batchelor, *The Doubleday Prayer Collection*, 95.

Godsequence

"But they and our ancestors acted presumptuously and stiffened their necks and did not obey your commandments; they refused to obey, and were not mindful of the wonders that you performed among them; but they stiffened their necks and determined to return to their slavery in Egypt. But you are a God ready to forgive, gracious and merciful, slow to anger and abounding in steadfast love, and you did not forsake them."

—Nehemiah 9:16–17

One of the great benefits of my vocation is to be able to witness miracles. I remember when I learned that one of my mentors had been diagnosed with a terminal illness; after a period of treatment and more prayers than anyone could number, he went into full remission. Another time, one of my parishioners, who was a politician early in life and by his own confession had made many enemies, was diagnosed with liver cancer and given only months to live. However, to the amazement of his doctors and family members, he actually lived over two years, which gave him the opportunity to make peace with everyone he had hurt during the darker season of his life.

Such miracles in the lives of others, but not in our own, may prompt us to think, "What about my friend, spouse, child, parent, or me? Does God love them more than me?" No.

Let me say it again. No.

Over my years of pastoral ministry, I have prayed with folks who had chronic or terminal illnesses, people who were, for a time, delivered from the disease and even certain death. I have also prayed with other people who got worse and eventually died. Why? Why do some seem to squeak by and some do not? Why do some get to cross the goal line and spike the ball and others leave the field altogether?

Let me offer a few caveats first before we tackle these questions. First, it is probably important to keep in mind that no one gets out of this world alive. Every person Jesus raised from the dead, even Lazarus, had to die again.

Second, I believe in miracles and I believe in the power of prayer to affect such miracles. But miracles do not always occur in the way I would like them to occur, and prayers are not always answered the way I would like them to be. For instance, I have had people with terminal illness tell me that they would receive their death as a miracle—a blessed release.

So back to that question. The Bible suggests to us that miracles have one purpose: to point us back to God. Scholars cannot seem to agree on who actually wrote the book of Nehemiah in the Hebrew Bible, but they are fairly certain it was the same person who wrote 1 and 2 Chronicles and the book of Ezra. The point of the series is to chronicle a specific period of ancient Israel's history. In the passage above, the author is writing to God about a time when the Jews, through a series of miracles, had been freed from Egyptian captivity. But no sooner had they been freed, they forgot the wonderful miracles God had done.

Miracles are not about you or me, who gets one and who does not. Miracles are about God. C.S. Lewis wrote, "Miracles in fact are retelling in small letters of the very same story which is written across the whole world in letters too large for some of us to see."[52] Miracles remind us that there is someone much bigger, much more important than us. They point us, again and again, to the God who created us, who redeems us, and who sustains us.

If we brush off a miracle as just a coincidence, then we have

---

52 C.S. Lewis, *God in the Dock*. Ed. Walter Hooper (Grand Rapids: Eerdmans, 1972), 29.

missed its point. As Archbishop William Temple said, "All I know is the more I pray, the more coincidences there are in my life." The more we pray, the more we have eyes to see; the more we have eyes to see, the more miracles become apparent. Some arrive with supernatural fanfare like healing, restoration of a broken marriage or friendship, or an insight that saves the business. Some arrive rather quietly like the small voice of friendship, the joy of a lover's kiss, the silence of the setting sun, and at times even death. As John Claypool used to tell me, "God is always changing water to wine, just a bit slower than at the wedding in Cana of Galilee." But, then there are the big ones—someone is healed, another escapes disaster, a business unexpectedly turns around—the list goes on.

I am grateful to be able to witness all kinds of miracles, which I believe not to be a consequence, but perhaps a Godsequence: a reminder that recipients of such gifts are not the only ones who are special to God; we all are.

— *Another Step . . .* —

When is the last time you witnessed a miracle? Maybe you are witnessing one now; watch for it.

A Prayer

I asked for strength that I might achieve;
I was made weak that I might learn humbly to obey.
I asked for health that I might do greater things;
I was given infirmity that I might do better things.
I asked for riches that I might be happy;
I was given poverty that I might be wise.
I asked for power that I might have the praise of men;
I was given weakness that I might feel the need of God.

I asked for all things that I might enjoy life;
I was given life that I might enjoy all things.
I got nothing that I had asked for,
But everything that I had hoped for.
Almost despite myself, my unspoken prayers were answered;
I am, among all men, most richly blessed.

—Unknown soldier, 1865[53]

---

53 Counsell, *2000 Years of Prayer*, 429–430.

Unforbidden Fruit

Beloved, let us love one another, because love is from
God; everyone who loves is born of God and knows
God. Whoever does not love does not know God, for
God is love. God's love was revealed among us in this
way: God sent His only Son into the world so that we
might live through Him. In this is love, not that we
loved God but that He loved us and sent His Son to be
the atoning sacrifice for our sins. Beloved, since God
loved us so much, we also ought to love one another.
No one has ever seen God; if we love one another, God
lives in us, and his love is perfected in us.
—1 John 4:7–12

I suppose we preachers are accused of spending more time than
necessary pointing out "forbidden fruits." As we saw a few meditations back, Paul lists the fruits of the Holy Spirit that are planted
in the heart of the Christian believer. Through God's grace and
our personal devotion, these fruits take root and grow. Tucked
into Paul's list is an unforbidden fruit: love.

Recently, I read back through what are known as John's Epistles
(1, 2, and 3 John). These are beautiful letters, written by the same
author of both John's gospel and the book of Revelation. As John
wrote these letters, the young church and its body of Christians
were beginning to feel the full brunt of persecution. John was clear
throughout his letters that it was important to be grounded in faith
and to be diligently weeding out evil both in one's individual life
and the church itself. It is interesting that soaked throughout these

letters of admonition is the constant call to live in love, express love, and to be children of love.

Facing a world that literally hated the followers of Jesus, John did not suggest a return of evil for evil, to take up arms, or even to turn away, but to continue to love.

> For this is the message you heard from the beginning, that we should love one another. . . . Do not be surprised, brothers and sisters, that the world hates you. . . . This is how we know love: Jesus Christ laid down his life for us—and we ought to lay down our lives for our brothers and sisters. . . . Dear children, let us not love with words or tongue but with actions and in truth.[54]

We have our day-to-day reasons for why we do not act in a loving way: we are tired or stressed, money is tight, the boss is on our back, we have a headache. We all have those moments, but when we fail to act in a loving way as a general characteristic, then something is amiss.

A deeper reason that we may fail to offer this unforbidden fruit to others is that we have forgotten how much we are loved. Unconditional and generous love is a remedy to virtually all our emotional and spiritual ills. When someone refuses to love, it is often because they have not experienced it themselves. Many people come from faulty and broken homes where real love was something bruised and bent at best. These people lose a sense of self-worth and security that would naturally come with an innate sense that regardless of anything, there is someone there who cares about them. Who cares about us.

Perhaps that is why John also writes, "See what love the Father has given us, that we should be called children of God; and that is what we are" (1 John 3:1). Oh, if we could let that good word sink down into our souls, then regardless of childhood, work

---

54 1 John 3:11, 13, 16, 18.

environment, or general disposition, we could begin to feast on, as well as share with others, the unforbidden fruit of love.

And what does love look like? The thirteenth chapter in the First Letter of Paul to the Corinthians is often called "The Love Chapter." You have probably heard parts of it read at weddings. As a description of love, Paul hits the nail on the head.

> Love is patient; love is kind; love is not envious or boastful or arrogant or rude. It does not insist on its own way; it is not irritable or resentful; it does not rejoice in wrongdoing but rejoices in the truth. It bears all things, believes all things, hopes all things, endures all things. Love never ends. (1 Corinthians 13:4–8a)

Pause for a moment and review the list. Is this how you express love to your friends, spouse, children, coworkers, or fellow church members? None of us can love perfectly; only one did so. But love should be growing in us; if it is not, then we need to go back to the source, Jesus Christ.

Have you opened your heart fully to Christ's love? Have you invited him to come and take up residence? Is he Lord and Savior, and not just somebody in Sunday school stories? If you can answer "Yes" to these questions, then love is planted and it will grow. But if the answer is "No" or "I'm not really sure," then perhaps it is time to allow Christ past the perimeter of your life and into its very core. Once you do, God's love will begin to nourish you and, in turn, you will be able to offer your own fruit basket to the hungry souls around you and feed them with that fruit that, thanks be to God, is unforbidden.

— *Another Step . . .* —

Have you, do you, experience the love of God? Do you know
how much God loves you? How can you more fully share
that love with others? If you are reticent to do so, what is it
that stops you?

A Prayer

O God, I seek a love that is already there; I want to
know a love that is already present; help me in my
frailty and self-centeredness to open my heart to your
love. Fill me afresh so that made whole with that love,
I may share it with all You send my way. In the name
of God, Whose other name is Love. *Amen.*

—RJL+

Tilling the Soil

Hear, O Israel: The Lord is our God, the Lord alone.
You shall love the Lord your God with all your heart,
and with all your soul, and with all your might. Keep
these words that I am commanding you today in your
heart.

—Deuteronomy 6:4–6

The passage above is known in Judaism as the great Shema—a
kind of singular law of the land that Moses impressed into the
minds of the Hebrew people who were making their way from
a life of bondage in Egypt to a life of freedom in the Promised
Land. Jesus pulled from the Shema one day when he was asked
which was the greatest of all laws. He responded, "'You shall love
the Lord your God with all your heart, and with all your soul,
and with all your mind.' This is the greatest and first commandment. And a second one is like it, 'You shall love your neighbor as
yourself.' On these two commandments hang all the law and the
prophets."[55]

As suggested in the last meditation, inviting that love into our
hearts is a good starting place for living out the law of love—that
"unforbidden fruit." But, as was also suggested, that fruit has a
tendency to grow when nurtured by a disciplined life of spiritual
devotion, which can happen in many ways. Over the next few
meditations, I want to focus on four: study of and humility before
the Bible, prayer, worship, and service. These are not listed in any
particular order. All of them require personal sacrifice, and a

---

55 Matthew 22:36–40; Mark 12:28–31.

willingness to both give up something and take something on. In a practical way, we must give up time—spend time—doing something that not many people in today's world fully appreciate. Also, in a submissive way, we must come seeking to receive what these acts of devotion may have for us. A submissive willingness to be moved, changed, taught, helped, comforted, afflicted, and finally transformed by the experiences of giving oneself to personal devotion is an important pathway to living in a way that honors God.

Before the Middle Ages, the only way farmers had to till the soil was with mules and thin, light rakes that just skimmed across the ground. This process, called "skittering," merely turned over the topsoil, such that when seeds were scattered, it was hard for them to set in and grow down. For obvious reasons, skittering yielded a fairly anemic harvest.

When iron became a more frequent piece of the agricultural landscape, large, heavy blades could be hauled behind not just one, but a team of oxen. The blades would go down deep and really turn over the soil. It was taxing work as farmers encountered rabbit holes, wasps' nests, and rocks and roots that made them have to stop and start over. They called the new method "deep plowing." It required longer hours and harder work, but then the seeds went down deeper where the soil was richer and, of course, the harvest was much more bountiful.

If we are willing to allow God's love to plow much deeper into our hearts, it may turn up old roots, stones, and wasps' nests, but once they are out of the way, that same love will grow much deeper. Of course, when that happens, the harvest is always plentiful.

— *Another Step . . .* —

As we prepare to look at just a few avenues of spiritual devotion, where do you feel the "brakes coming on"? Where do you feel resistance? Why? Why do you think that is the case?

A Prayer

Now it is You alone that I love,
You alone that I follow,
You alone that I seek,
You alone that I feel ready to serve,
Because You alone rule justly,
It is to Your authority alone that I want to submit,
Command me, I pray, to do whatever You will,
But heal and open my ears
That I may hear Your voice.
Heal and open my eyes
That I may see Your will,
Drive out from me
All fickleness,
That I may acknowledge You alone.
Tell me where to look
That I may see You,
And I will place my hope in doing Your will.
Amen.

—St. Augustine, d. 430[56]

56 Batchelor, *The Doubleday Prayer Collection*, 395.

To Pray

He was praying in a certain place, and after he had finished, one of his disciples said to him, "Lord, teach us to pray, as John taught his disciples." He said to them, "When you pray, say: Father, hallowed be your name. Your kingdom come. Give us each day our daily bread. And forgive us our sins, for we ourselves forgive everyone indebted to us. And do not bring us to the time of trial."

—Luke 11:1–4

One way in which we begin to more deeply break the topsoil of our lives so that God can do a bit of deep planting within us is prayer. Prayer, that crucial link of communication between human and the Divine, is one of the primary ways that God speaks to us and we can speak to Him. In my vocation, I have found that people pray in all kinds of ways, places, and with all kinds of words and actions. I have included in these meditations a kind of hodge-podge of prayers from a variety of Christians. A quick skim would show you the kind of variety that I mean. I do not think the how, where, and why is nearly as important as the simple do.

My wife and I recently toured a traveling Titanic exhibit. It tells once again that infamous and ominous story through a collection of photos and many actual artifacts that were scooped up from the ocean's floor in the north Atlantic. Plates looking as if they just came out of a dishwasher, clothes, a chandelier, tuxedo buttons, and a child's toy plane. Also included was a piece of sheet music, stained with salt water, but the title and most of the words could still be read.

On the sheet was a song that many believed was included in the
collection of pieces played by the now well-known string quartet
that performed even as the ship began its descent. The words at
the heading, "Teach Us to Pray." My guess is that there were many
that were praying on that desperate night. Perhaps some who were
quite familiar with the language of prayer, some who prayed every
now and then, some who were thinking, "Teach us to pray." Here
is the text attributed to James Montgomery:

> Lord, teach us how to pray aright
> Lord, teach us how to pray aright,
> with reverence and with fear;
> though dust and ashes in thy sight,
> we may, we must draw near.
> We perish if we cease from prayer,
> O grant us power to pray!
> And when to meet thee we prepare,
> Lord, meet us by the way.
> God of all grace, we bring to thee
> a broken, contrite heart;
> give, what thine eye delights to see,
> truth in the inward part.
> Faith in the only sacrifice
> that can for sin atone;
> to build our hopes, to fix our eyes,
> on Christ, on Christ alone;
> Patience to watch and wait and weep,
> though mercy long delay;
> courage our fainting souls to keep,
> and trust thee though thou slay.
> Give these, and then thy will be done;
> thus strengthened with all might,
> we through thy Spirit and thy Son,
> shall pray, and pray aright.[57]

---

57 Poem by James Montgomery, 1819.

In our verses for this devotion, Jesus responds to an inquiry about prayer with the words, "When you pray"—not "If you pray," or "When you get around to praying," but "When you pray." Prayer was an expectation and part of the business of being a disciple. As Philip Yancey notes,

> The psychiatrist Gerald C. May observed, "After twenty years of listening to the yearnings of people's hearts, I am convinced that human beings have an inborn desire for God. Whether we are consciously religious or not, this desire is our deepest longing and most precious treasure." Surely, if we are made in God's own image, God will find a way to fulfill that deepest longing. Prayer is that way.[58]

We need not wait for an emergency to turn to prayer; we must continue to foster the language of prayer daily as one of those open doors to a deeper relationship with our Lord. The apostles were not alone in their desire to know how to pray. Maybe we are more like them than we realize.

So, not if, but when you pray, you might need a little help along the way. On your knees is a good place to start, then begin as the apostles did, "Lord, teach us to pray." Indeed, "We perish if we cease from prayer, O grant us power to pray!"

— *Another Step . . .* —

The devotional writer Richard Foster has said, "To pray is to change." What change might prayer bring to your life?

---

58 Philip Yancey, *Prayer: Does It Make Any Difference?* (Grand Rapids: Zondervan, 2006), 16.

A Prayer

Let us not seek out of thee what we can find only in thee, O Lord: peace and rest and joy and bliss, which abide in thee alone.

Lift up our souls above the weary round of harassing thoughts to Thy eternal presence.

Lift up our minds to the pure, bright, serene, light of Thy presence, that there we may repose in Thy love and be at rest from ourselves and all things that weary us; and thence return, arrayed in Thy peace, to do and to bear whatsoever shall best please thee, O blessed Lord.

—The Reverend Canon E. B. Pusey, d. 1882[59]

---

59 Batchelor, *The Doubleday Prayer Collection*, 410.

God-Breathed

All scripture is inspired by God and is useful for
teaching, for reproof, for correction, and for training in
righteousness, so that everyone who belongs to God
may be proficient, equipped for every good work.

—2 Timothy 3:16–17

In the denomination I serve, one of the most moving of all litur-
gical services is the ordination of a deacon or priest into the service of the church. To me, one of the most moving pieces of that
particular service is when the candidate must pledge, in front of
the entire congregation, "I solemnly declare that I do believe the
Holy Scriptures of the Old and New Testaments to be the Word
of God and to contain all things necessary to salvation."[60] After
those words the candidate must, in the presence of all gathered,
sign a document that attests to the spoken promise.

In addition to prayer, one of the ways God speaks to us is
through the Holy Scriptures of the Bible. We call them "holy"
because they are, indeed, set apart from all other writings. Every
now and then I encounter someone who says something along the
lines of, "I don't know why you make such a big deal about the
Bible; it's just a book like any other, written by humans." To buy
into that kind of thinking would require that I turn my back on
the crucial promise I made at my own ordination; it also shows an
arrogant irreverence for the book that has played such a large part
in the revelation of our faith and our God.

---

60 Book of Common Prayer, 538.

Humans tend to take great pride in our own knowledge. As with prayer, to rest our minds and souls before scripture requires an element of humility. Many modern people tend to believe that God treats all modes of revelation equally—poetry, nature, music, literature, theater, even television and film. In part that is true, because God's revelation can be made known in and through many avenues. But Christians must take a different view of God's revelation through Holy Scripture. The Bible serves as the ethical, moral, theological, and spiritual compass for the Christian. Without that compass we are very likely to lose our way and stray far from the path of the Christian journey.

Richard Hooker, a kind of architect of early Protestant faith as it was expressed through Anglicanism, wrote, "What Scripture doth plainly deliver, to that the first place both of credit and obedience is due; the next whereunto is whatsoever any man can necessarily conclude by force of reason: after these the voice of the church succeedeth."[61] In other words, when it comes to receiving scripture, it speaks plainly first for itself and then can make its way to the lens of human reason and the voice of the church.

A moving moment of this view of Holy Scripture played out during the coronation of Queen Elizabeth I. Though arguably the most powerful monarch of her time, as a symbol of her submission to the Bible, she ordered that, "[A] Bible, translated into English, let down to her on a silken cord by a child representing Truth. Elizabeth, ever mindful of the visually dramatic, kissed both her hands as she reached out to receive it and then kissed the Bible itself and clasped it to her breast. She promised the expectant crowd she would study and learn from it."[62]

Thus, we Christians are called to read Holy Scripture as another avenue to knowing God, and allowing God to move in and dwell in us more securely. If we want to know God, it is important to read God's Word. The literal translation of Paul's words from his letter to Timothy cited in the opening verses is that "all Scripture

---

61 *Ecclesiastical Polity*, 1593–1597.
62 Jane Dunn, *Elizabeth and Mary: Cousins, Rivals, Queens* (New York: Vintage, 2005), 32.

is God-breathed." Wow. In other words, it is a kind of love letter from the Holy One to humankind itself. It tells the story again and again, in so many ways: the story of creation, struggle, sin, redemption, and hope for humanity.

The modern Christian will wisely see that some of scripture is literally true—some is history, some instruction, some letters written from one saint to another. We also acknowledge that some of scripture is inspired truth spoken through story, metaphor, and imagery. We can affirm that some of scripture applies only to the audience to whom it was addressed or the time in which it was written, and that some of it is just as timely for Christians now as it was the day ink was put to parchment. What the modern Christian cannot do, if they wish to live a Christian life, is to set the Bible on the shelf next to the dictionary and photo albums, to be pulled out only in moments of spiritual desperation.

I have had members of the parishes I have served say to me that they do not read the Bible because they "do not understand it," or "it is too tedious," or "its language is too difficult." Our excuses for not reading Holy Scripture must be stripped away from the truth like a wrapper from a valuable present. The Bible addresses our issues of relationships, loneliness, anxiety, emptiness, fear, finances, sexuality, work ethic, taxes, and so much more. Theodore Roosevelt wrote, "If a man is not familiar with the Bible, he has suffered a loss which he had better make all possible haste to correct."

Catholic monastic Thomas Merton unveiled his own view of scripture with these words, "By reading of scripture, I am so renewed that all nature seems renewed around me and with me. The sky seems to be a purer, cooler blue, the trees a deeper green, light is sharper on the outlines of the forest and the hills and the whole world is charged with the glory of God."[63]

Ambrose wrote, "As in Paradise, God walks in the Holy Scriptures, seeking the human being." How can you learn to seek God in the Bible? Call your pastor or priest. Attend a Bible study.

---

63 These quotes were taken from personal notes kept throughout the author's ministry.

Perhaps most importantly, pick up the Bible and read it daily. Read it slowly, a chapter at a time or maybe just a paragraph at a time. Start simply, perhaps with the Psalms or one of the gospels. The key is to start. The good news is, if you jump in there and begin to read, the seeking part is over and you get to walk along with the Holy One who is already walking along with you.

— *Another Step . . .* —

Read Psalm 1. What does this ancient hymn say to you? If you can find some insight into God in this one piece, do you not think there is much more to learn?

A Prayer

Blessed Lord, who hast caused all Holy Scriptures
to be written for our learning: Grant that we may in
such wise hear them, read, mark, learn, and inwardly
digest them; that by patience and comfort of thy holy
Word, we may embrace and ever hold fast the blessed
hope of everlasting life, which thou hast given us in
our Savior Jesus Christ; who liveth and reigneth with
thee and the Holy Spirit, one God, forever and ever.
Amen.[64]

—From the Book of Common Prayer

---

64 Book of Common Prayer, 184.

In Holy Splendor

O Lord, our Sovereign, how majestic is Your name in
all the earth! You have set your glory above the earth!

—Psalm 8:1

A few pages back we took some time to look at idolatry, particularly as it reflects a misplaced allegiance in the affections of our
heart. One of the ways Christians, and our Jewish forebearers,
reflected their allegiance was the act of participatory worship.
And the first step of worship is showing up.

We are told in Luke 4:16 that Jesus went to synagogue, "as was
his custom." My guess is that there were days when the sermon
went on a bit too long, someone was hacking away with a cough
in the back pew, or the reader stumbled on his words, but Jesus
still showed up.

Worship is a reflection of those things in which we place our
worth. If our relationship with Christ is important to us, then we
will certainly show up. If we knew the Queen of England would
be in church next Sunday, would we scramble to get a seat? What
if our favorite film star, sports figure, or author were speaking—
would we make an extra effort to be there?

God who shows up every week—the Creator of the universe, the
Redeemer of humankind—meets us in worship. Of course, there
are days when it may seem like God may not be there because the
sermon is boring, the sound system isn't working, or the hymns
may be unfamiliar. But worship is more than the "how"; it centers
on the "who." If knowing Jesus matters to us, then spending time
in worshipping him matters as well.

Every now and then, someone comes up to me after worship and says, "I don't like that hymn," or "I really don't like that communion prayer," or "I prefer a different version of the Bible." Notice what all those statements have in common? "I." As a worship leader, I want to be attentive to things that turn the worshipper off from drawing closer to God, and I also want to help people remember that worship is about Christ, not about the congregation.

As James Torrance puts it, "When we focus on the question of who, we can rejoice together as we look away from ourselves to Him, that He may sanctify us and lead us together into the presence of the Holy Father."[65] Thus, an important element in worship is making sure we do not think so much about what I want, but focus, instead, on Jesus. Then, perhaps, we will find eyes to see how the words, hymns, music, and liturgy are an expression of our love for him.

I know some may ask, "Can't I just do all of this at home?" I recently read a Victorian scene when a clergyman went to call on one of his members who had stopped going to church. They were sitting in front of a roaring fire when the parishioner said, "Why can't I just stay at home and worship God in my own way?" Without saying a word, the priest went over to the fire, opened the screen, and began to separate the piled-up coals that were providing the light and warmth of the fire. He moved each one out from another until they all sat alone along the grate. As he did, the fire began to die down, and the warmth in the room nearly went away. His parishioner got the point and showed up again the next week.

Like prayer and like reading of Holy Scripture, worship is a matter of acting on our desire to be an authentic disciple of Jesus Christ. It gives us an opportunity to brush up to God's presence. David, the author of so many of our wonderful hymns, poems, and songs of praise, reminds God's people that this brushing up

---

65 James B. Torrance, *Worship, Community & the Triune God of Grace* (New York: InterVarsity, 1997), 92.

against God is one of those heart-shifting experiences that grows out of worship: "Ascribe to the Lord the glory due his name; bring an offering, and come before Him. Worship the Lord in holy splendor; tremble before him, all the earth" (1 Chronicles 16:29–30). Worship gives us the opportunity to allow that fire of Christ to burn just a bit brighter within us and around us. Just go sit, kneel, listen, pray, recite. Let it be your custom, as it was for Jesus. When you do gather, remember that it is about him.

—— *Another Step . . .* ——

What, if anything, keeps you from being a regular partici-pant in worship? What is the real reason? If you do worship on a regular basis, how can you more fully invest yourself in the experience?

A Prayer

Almighty God, we will come into Thy house, even upon the multitude of thy mercies, and in Thy fear will we worship toward Thy holy Temple. Hear the voice of our humble petitions, when we cry unto Thee, when we hold up our hands towards Thy mercy-seat. Let Thine eyes be open, and let Thine ears be attentive to hearken unto the prayer which Thy servants pray toward the place, whereof Thou hast said, that Thou wouldest put thy name there; for the sake of Jesus Christ. *Amen.*

—Lancelot Andrewes, d. 1626
Bishop of Chichester, Ely and Winchester[66]

---

66 Counsell, *2000 Years of Prayer,* 229.

Let the Service Begin

"When the Son of Man comes in his glory, and all
the angels with him, then he will sit on the throne
of his glory. All the nations will be gathered before
him, and he will separate people one from another
as a shepherd separates the sheep from the goats,
and he will put the sheep on his right hand and the
goats at the left. Then the king will say to those at his
right hand, 'Come you that are blessed by my Father,
inherit the kingdom prepared for you from the foun-
dation of the world; for I was hungry and you gave
me food, I was thirsty and you gave me something to
drink, I was a stranger and you welcomed me, I was
naked and you gave me clothing, I was sick and you
visited me. . . . Truly I tell you, just as you did it to one
of the least of these who are members of my family,
you did it to me.'"

—Matthew 25:31–36, 40

For five years of my ordained ministry I served a wonderful parish
in Lafayette, Louisiana. It was my first season as a rector, so years
of study and apprenticeship were now going to have to come forward to present themselves as practical and applicable.

Having spent my entire life up to that point east of the
Mississippi, I was (primarily due to my own lack of preparation)
thrust into what many know to be a unique culture. It is one
thing to eat and enjoy Cajun cuisine or listen and dance to zydeco
music. It is quite another to move to the region that birthed them.
I did not know what boudin or cracklins were. I had never seen

a nutria or an armadillo, much less in my front yard. I had never lived in a city where names like Melancon and Boudreaux were more common than Smith and Jones. The parish was very different in its style, size, and programs from any of the parishes I had previously assisted, but I was called to serve there and that is what I had to find a way to do: serve.

The prayer, Bible study, and worship we do to open ourselves more to the transforming power of the Holy Spirit should do more than color our beliefs and morals. It should call us to serve others. Service of any kind that is good and holy requires that we get out of ourselves and give of ourselves—that is the message unfolding in the verses from Matthew which offer a broad-brush portrait of the end of time that scholars call apocalyptic literature. Jesus tells His followers that following him means serving the hungry, the thirsty, the stranger, the naked, those in prison, and so on. When we serve others who are in need, we are serving him.

My first year in Lafayette was a real test of what I had learned in my years of graduate and post-graduate school, and in the relatively safe world of assistantship on a church staff. I could no longer blame others for the direction of the church; I was in the chair that ultimately had to steer the ship one way or another. What I learned, like any sailor will tell you, is that you cannot steer from the bow. The direction of the ship is determined by a captain who steers from the stern—where the rudder is. In other words, I had to be willing to go to the back of the line and serve. I had to give up some of my preconceived and prejudiced notions about the kinds of things I thought would work. I was in a different culture and I had to get my own proclivities out of the way and make space for those whom I was to serve.

I did not lose my personality or temperament, nor did I give up my morals or core beliefs. I did learn how to step back and remember that it was not what "I" wanted that mattered most, but what the person I encountered needed. That should be the kind of fruit our personal faith should produce. James put it well: "So faith by itself, if it has no works, is dead" (James 2:17).

Author Gayle Erwin reminds her readers that there are two central seas in Palestine. One is fresh and teeming with life surrounded by lush trees and playing children—it is alive. The River Jordan, she points out, feeds this sea with flowing water from the nearby hills. The Jordan flows into another sea where no fish can live and no song birds are heard. Neither animal nor human will drink from it.

What makes the mighty difference between these neighboring seas fed by the same river? The Sea of Galilee receives, but does not keep the Jordan. For every drop that flows into it, another drop flows out. What goes into the sea goes out in equal measure.

"The other sea is shrewder, hoarding its income jealously. It will not be tempted into any generous impulse. Every drop it gets it keeps," she writes. "The Sea of Galilee gives and lives. . . . The other sea gives nothing. It is named The Dead Sea. There are two kinds of people in the world. There are two seas in Palestine."[67]

Jesus lays it out much like Erwin. He says there are two kinds of people. Some are like sheep that know that because they have been tended to by a loving shepherd, one of their responsibilities is to serve beyond themselves. They know that with the gift of faith comes the responsibility of serving deeds. Then there are goats who, like the Dead Sea, hold on to what they have. Goats who, either deliberately or through inertia, refuse to serve are just about as useful to Christ as the Dead Sea is to its surroundings.

What I learned in Lafayette was to let go and serve the people God brought my way. I had plenty of days when I did not serve; the old selfish habits always die hard. But I found that when I shared the gifts God had given me in service to God and God's children, I drew closer to them and to him. Every drop I relinquished, God replaced.

67 J. John and Mark Stibbe, comp. *A Box of Delights* (London: Monarch, 2001), 178.

I like the story of the woman who shows up just after the worship procession has headed down the center aisle of her church. When her tardiness brought her face to face with the priest who was last in the procession, she feigned ignorance and said, "Oh, I am sorry, pastor, when does the service begin?" He smiled and whispered, "The service begins when the worship is over."

— *Another Step . . .* —

Prayer, study of the scriptures, worship, and service are four ways that God can more effectively pour His Holy Spirit into us. As you review Jesus's list of opportunities to serve Him— is there one that really tugs at your heart? Are you called to a ministry of service to the hungry, the poor, the lonely, the imprisoned? Someone far away, someone close to home, or perhaps even someone in your home? How are you called to serve?

A Prayer

If we pray
   we will believe
If we believe
   we will love
If we love
   we will serve.
Only then can we put
   our love for God
   into living action
Through service of Christ
   in the distressing
   disguise of the Poor.
   —Mother Teresa of Calcutta, d. 1997[68]

68 Kathryn Spink, comp. *In the Silence of the Heart, Meditations by Mother Teresa* (London: SPCK, 1983).

Serious Business

Then He said to them all, "If any want to become my followers, let them deny themselves and take up their cross daily and follow me. For those who want to save their life will lose it, and those who lose their life for my sake will save it."

—Luke 9:23–24

A friend once challenged me by saying, "If you want to know what your priorities are, look at your calendar and your checkbook." This is true of both our relationships and our allegiances. I, like many of you, know people who spend far more of their time, talents, and financial resources on other non-profits than they do on Christ's work through their church family, which probes me to ask, "How seriously are we to take Christianity?" My hunch is very seriously.

When Jesus began his ministry, it centered around calling and welcoming new followers to travel along with him. The longer they traveled, the more difficult the road became. Jesus did not shy away from transparency. As his ministry headed toward its earthly end, he told his disciples things would not only get tougher, but they would get tougher by the day. "Take up the cross daily" were the words Jesus used to give fair warning. Serious, serious business.

It is fairly common to make Christianity merely an intellectual debate about various views of the Almighty, or a social experiment wherein we tackle the societal ills of the world under the banner of Christ. Faith gets stuck being lived out in our heads and our bodies, losing its way to our hearts and souls. I can prove my intellectual stamina and my social concern—those are fairly admirable in our world today—but to begin speaking of loving God with heart and soul may be taking it all a bit too far. Yet that is the deep call of Christ. I heard Former Archbishop Donald Coggan remark with great sadness, "The journey from head to heart is one of the longest and most difficult that we know."

If we are indeed serious about Christianity, then we need to go deeper than just knowing more or doing more. Following Christ does not mean imitating him, for we are not the same. Following Christ means loving him, drawing on him, allowing him to enter our lives such that not only are minds and wills transformed, but hearts and souls as well. That is why the metaphor of "new birth," which Jesus used and to which I have already referred, is so perfect. Christ came to call us out of our selfish tendencies to a life of selfless sacrifice. It is in that place that true joy and peace are found.

Anglican theologian Alister McGrath writes:

> [Christian] Spirituality is all about the way in which we encounter and experience God, and the transformation of our consciousness and our lives as a result of that encounter and experience. It is most emphatically not the exclusive preserve of some spiritual elite, preoccupied with unhealthy perfectionist tendencies. It is the common duty and joy of all Christian believers, as they long to enter into the deeper fellowship with the living God which is promised in the Scriptures. We can think of it in terms of the internalization of our faith. It means allowing our faith to saturate every aspect of our lives, infecting and affecting our thinking, feeling, and living.[69]

It was not merely Jesus's impact on the minds and bodies of His disciples that set them aflame with passion for God, but the transformation of their hearts and souls as well. So much so that each was willing to give up life if called upon to do so.

---

69 Alister McGrath, "Loving God with Heart and Mind," *Knowing and Doing*, Winter 2002.

How seriously should one take Christianity? I think we know. Perhaps a better question is, "How seriously do I take Christianity?" To find your answer, look at your calendar and your checkbook; you can even look to your mind and your body. But perhaps the real answer rests in looking even deeper into heart and soul.

With God's help, may the journey from head to heart happen in each of us.

—— *Another Step . . .* ——

How seriously do you take Christianity and the claims of Christ?

A Prayer

Lord Jesus Christ,
take all my freedom,
my memory, my understanding, and my will.
All that I have and cherish
You have given me.
I surrender it all to be guided by Your will.
Your grace and Your love are wealth enough for me.
Give me these, Lord Jesus,
And I ask for nothing more.

—Prayer of Self-Dedication to
Jesus Christ from *The Roman Missal*

Whom Will You Serve?

"Now therefore revere the Lord, and serve him in sincerity and in faithfulness; put away the gods that your ancestors served beyond the River and in Egypt, and serve the Lord. Now if you are unwilling to serve the Lord, choose this day whom you will serve, whether the gods of your ancestors served in the region beyond the River or the gods of the Amorites in whose land you are living; but as for me and my household, we will serve the Lord."

—Joshua 24:14–15

The passage above comes from one of the most well-known speeches in the entire Judeo-Christian story. It is often referred to as the "Covenant Renewal at Shechem." The long journey out of bondage in Egypt had come to its end and the faithful Hebrews were gathered. Moses's apprentice, Joshua, reminded them of their great history as a people freed from slavery who traversed the desert for decades, received God's Ten Commandments, and who, after such a long journey, had battled the Canaanites and were now laying claim to a land promised to them.

The climax of his speech is not the retelling of their history, but a question: "Now that God has seen you this far, will you go the rest of the way with him?" They, like you and me, had many options of who they could follow: idols, gods, personal interests, and pleasures. But Joshua put it to them: "Now therefore revere the Lord." Some translations suggest the word *revere* is actually more accurately translated as *fear*: "Before you make up your mind, fear the Lord."

"[People] who fear God face life fearlessly," wrote Richard Christian Halverson. "[People] who do not fear God end up fearing everything,"[70] Fear of God does not mean cowardice or anxiety before God, but "awe, honor, respect." For years, my aunt served as the Chief Justice of the Circuit Court of Appeals in the Commonwealth of Virginia. All of my life, I had known her as Aunt Jo, an easygoing, good-humored, loving mother, aunt, and wife. During my graduate study in Northern Virginia, we lived not too far from my aunt and her place of service.

One day, my wife and I decided to visit her courtroom. She was in her black robe, attorneys lined up to see her. She literally held court. When she spoke, everyone's attention turned to her; she was master and commander of that piece of Virginia real estate. Whoever was in the room, whether attorney, plaintiff, or defendant, found it necessary to fear my Aunt Jo. She was the one in control. So it goes with God. We are to fear him, in the sense that when it comes to all we call Creation, God is the boss. That we live in relationship with our Creator should fill us with awe and respect.

When we our focus shifts from God to humankind, we will slowly descend into a fear that does not incorporate awe and honor, but anxiety. This kind of fear is the root cause of so many of our human disorders and sin. This kind of fear gives birth in us to a deep sense that there is not enough to go around, whether that be material things (causing us to hoard or steal) or non-material things (causing us to either withhold our love or desperately seek it in wrong and harmful ways).

John speaks to one remedy for the second kind of fear: "There is no fear in love, but perfect love casts out fear" (1 John 4:18). When we know, deep down, that we are perfectly and fully loved, what is drawn out of us is that sick, gnawing kind of fear. The path to that kind of freedom from fear is to fear God. As John Witherspoon said, "It is only the fear of God that can deliver us from the fear of [humanity]." The real call is to let God have his rightful place in our lives as Lord and Savior personified in Christ

---

70 Manser, *The Westminster Collection of Christian Quotations*, 110.

Jesus. Then, the fears that plague our hearts and lives will melt like ice in the warm sun.

Of what are you afraid? Does it not help to know there is someone who loves you more than anyone walking the earth? That one does, indeed, deserve our fear and awe. There is comfort in that kind of love. In fact, that kind of love really does cast out fear. As Charles Wesley wrote: "Jesus! The name that charms our fears; that bids our sorrows cease; 'Tis music in the sinner's ear, 'Tis life, and health, and peace!"[71]

Let's go back to Shechem. Perhaps Joshua should have just cut to the chase and said, "God has carried you this far because he loves you, now think about that for a minute. You know the two choices out there, fear or God. Whom will you serve?"

— *Another Step . . .* —

Of what are you more afraid, not being loved by God or loving God? If you know you are loved by Him, then do you still have a need to fear?

A Prayer

At times Lord, I forget Your love for me. And, there are times I ignore it and turn from it. When I fail to receive Your love, then I find that great darkness creeping over me—with all its angst, and pain, and anxiety—all of its fear.

Help me, dear Jesus Christ, to allow You to cast aside anything that stands between Your love and me. Help me to fear You as our forebears did, so that in fearing You, I may have no fear, and at life's long end, know and receive Your perfect love.

—RJL+

71 *The Hymnal 1982* (New York: The Church Hymnal Corporation, 1982), 493.

Blessed Is the King

... throwing their cloaks on the colt, they set Jesus on it. As he rode along, people kept spreading their cloaks on the road. As he was now approaching the path down from the Mount of Olives, the whole multitude of the disciples began to praise God joyfully with a loud voice for all the deeds of power they had seen, saying, "Blessed is the king who comes in the name of the Lord! Peace in heaven, and glory in the highest heaven!" Some of the Pharisees in the crowd said to Him, "Teacher, order your disciples to stop." He answered, "I tell you, if these were silent, the stones would shout out."

—Luke 19:35–40

If you have been using this book as a Lenten companion, you are beginning Holy Week—those seven days between Palm Sunday and Easter Sunday. If it is a companion for another time of year, I invite you still to consider how this week we call "holy" through the traditions of our faith still speaks.

The scene above is called the Triumphal Entry. Matthew's gospel adds the color green to the story by telling that people did not just fling cloaks on the ground in front of the donkey that carried Jesus, but waved palm branches in celebration. Despite the obvious jubilation, a shadow hung over the moment when the religious leaders told Jesus to have his followers pipe down. You can imagine Jesus replying with a gentle smile, "You know guys, even if I told them to put a lid on it, the little stones at our feet would start to do their own chorus of praise." As the week went, the shadow grew longer and darker.

It is a strange turn of events. At the beginning of the week, the crowd is cheering Jesus; in no time, things begin to head south. Only days later, virtually everyone who wanted to be near Jesus on that first Palm Sunday wanted nothing to do with him by the time Good Friday rolled around.

Following the Triumphal Entry, Jesus offered a few more salient teachings, healings, then he met betrayal, a trial, torture, and crucifixion. We would like to bypass all of the pain and go straight to the good news of Easter Sunday, but we just cannot have a resurrection without a death. In the next few meditations, we will explore different aspects of holiness and Holy Week.

Perhaps one of the most famous Palm Sunday hymns is one entitled, "All Glory Laud and Honor." The story goes that when Charlemagne died, his son, Louis I, assumed the throne of his mighty father. All went well until he began to divide up the massive kingdom, and then it all began to fall apart. He never enjoyed the security of the throne his father had known. Caught in the middle of all of this was Theodulph, Bishop of Orleans, a city in the south of France. He was an incredible leader who worked hard to reform the clergy, establish schools, advance education, and build churches. He was a brilliant and moral man who also composed hymns. But, during the intrigues of Louis's reign, Theodulph was falsely accused of siding against his monarch. He was imprisoned on Easter Sunday. Tradition says that Louis visited the place of Theodulph's imprisonment and halted outside the bishop's window, who in return sang this well-known hymn that he, himself, wrote while in that prison. The king was so moved that he immediately ordered the bishop's release.

Originally, there were seventy-eight verses to the hymn. Rarely are all of them sung today, but they are a reminder of how hopeless things do not always have the last word. What faith he must have had to write these words in the darkness of a prison.

All glory, laud, and honor, To Thee, Redeemer King,
To whom the lips of children, Made sweet hosannas ring.

Somehow the acknowledgement of those first hosannas to our
King's trek toward Good Friday, in the end, meant release for the
bishop. It can for each of us as well.

So, let us begin our descent toward the Cross with Bishop
Theodulph's hymn. Let us even travel to the darkness of his cell
and ponder our own Lord's descent. Let us hold in our hearts the
promises that in keeping our eyes fixed on Christ, there will be
sweet release in the story's end, or perhaps, beginning.

— *Another Step . . .* —

Some define the word *holy* as meaning "set apart." What is
holy to you? If the days ahead are to be treated as a "holy
week," what can you do to personally make it set apart from
all other weeks?

A Prayer
Dear Master, we remember that many who claimed
you as King on Sunday shouted "crucify" on Friday.
So confirm our faith today that our love for you will
never falter or turn to hatred but will remain constant
now and forever. We offer our worship to you, Lord,
with all our love. *Amen.*[72]

72 Hazel Snashall, comp. *Prayers before Worship* (Lawrenceville, NJ: National Christian
Education Council, 1984).

Dealing with the Cover-Up

Then the eyes of both were opened, and they knew
that they were naked; and they sewed fig leaves
together and made loincloths for themselves. They
heard the sound of the Lord God walking in the
garden at the time of the evening breeze, and the
man and his wife hid themselves from the presence
of the Lord God among the trees of the garden.

—Genesis 3:7–8

We began our journey talking a good bit about death and sin, and
we are going to circle back as we head toward a conclusion. It is
true that when God created all the wonderful pieces of the earth,
he ended the majestic project by saying, "It is very good."[73]

That truth that springs from the story of the Garden of Eden
is important. God set humankind free, but warned them that disobedience carried the price of sin and death. All was good and
well, but somewhere along the line, Adam and Eve spent too much
time with the serpent. They ate, they fell, sin entered, and it all
came unraveled. The good turned sour.

Whenever the above passage is read in church, I usually
encounter a member who has to comment, perhaps with a little
grin, on that "naked" business. The grin is there I suppose, to hide
the bit of discomfort we may feel thinking about the first humans
out there in the Garden without a stitch on. What was going on?

Adam and Eve knew they had done something wrong in the
same way a child quickly snaps his hand out of the cookie jar and

---

73 Genesis 1:31.

begins whistling when Mom enters the room. Adam and Eve were dealing with their own guilt by drawing attention away from who they were created to be (naked, pure, innocent) to whom they had become (red-faced, caught, shamed). God left that curse of covering nakedness as a kind of reminder that we always should be, with his help, working back toward our innocence and nakedness.

Several years ago, I was fortunate to spend some time in Japan. My Japanese was pretty much limited to words like, "Please," "Thank you," "Excuse me," and "Which way to the bathroom?" I have learned that the Japanese have two words to describe how humans present themselves to the world. The first is *tatemae* or "the part of myself that I let the world see," and the second is *hon ne* or "that place on the inside where no one can see." Philip Yancey suggests that perhaps we need a third word for the secret places that we never make known to anyone. I am suggesting to you that it is that third place that God is trying to get to, open up, heal, and make known. God wants more than just the faces we give to the world: God also wants the one that we try to hide. Yancey confesses,

> In vain I sometimes build barriers to keep God out, stubbornly disregarding the fact that God looks on the heart, penetrating beyond the tatemae and hon ne to where no person can see. As God informed the prophet Samuel, "The Lord does not look at the things man looks at. Man looks at the outward appearance, but the Lord looks at the heart."[74]

As my mentor John Stott likes to say, "What happened in the Garden was the first instance of a cover-up." I wonder what would have happened if, rather than reach for the fig leaves, Adam and Eve just fessed up, waited in the Garden, and when God returned, admitted in all their nakedness and shame what they had done. Surely, in some sense, they would have restored honesty with God about who they were and about how much they needed God not

74 Yancey, *Prayer*, 46; 1 Samuel 16:7.

just when everything was good, but also when things went terribly wrong.

We need that honesty, too. The journey between Palm Sunday and Easter Sunday is a good season to lay bare before God what is going on inside. If we strip away the clothes of pretense before God, perhaps even before others, we can be available to one another and, of course, to God.

There is much in today's world to give others the impression that we are superbly self-sufficient. But often, only we and God know what is going on behind closed doors. When we strip off the outer shell, the clothes if you will, real intimacy and authentic love can take place. Pause. Take some time to be honest with God; do not let him just see your game face, but all your faces. Invite God into not just your public garden, but the private one as well. Let God show you where the weeds are, where new growth is needed, what needs to be pruned, and what needs to be tended. If you do, you will find yourself come Easter morning emerging from whatever tomb you may face today.

— *Another Step . . .* —

What is one thing you are hiding (or think you are hiding) from God right now that really needs to be laid bare before him?

A Prayer

O Lord, I have sinn'd, and the black number swells
To such a dismal sum,
That should my stony heart and eyes,
And this whole sinful trunk a flood become,
And melt to tears, their drops could not suffice
To count my score,
Much less to pay

But thou, my God, hast blood in store,
Yet, since the balsam of thy blood,
Although it can, will do no good,
Unless the wound be cleans'd in tears before;
Thou in whose sweet, but pensive face,
Laughter could never steal a place,
Teach but my heart and eyes
To melt away,
And then one drop of balsam will suffice.

—Jeremy Taylor, d. 1667
Bishop of Down and Connor
Vice-Chancellor of Dublin University[75]

75 Counsell, *2000 Years of Prayer*, 276–277.

The Black Bean

"... he has appeared once for all at the end of the age
to remove sin by the sacrifice of himself. And just as
it is appointed for mortals to die once, and after that
the judgment, so Christ, having been offered once to
bear the sins of many, will appear a second time, not
to deal with sin, but to save those who are eagerly
waiting for him."

—Hebrews 9:26–28

Not only did shame and guilt grow out of the disobedience of those first humans, but death did as well. God's intent was that life would reign, but sin brought death into the picture, along with things like decay and rust. As much as we wince at the thought, each of us has been grafted into the family that must face a final day.

My wife and I are Texans now. Any good Texan soon learns he or she has to make a kind of Lone Star pilgrimage to the Alamo, which we did within weeks of our move across the state's border. The trip to the nexus of history and tragedy was humbling and disquieting. It reminded me of my first trip to the USS Arizona's "remains" in Pearl Harbor nearly four decades ago.

The familiar battle cry, "Remember the Alamo," and the tragic events that haunt those hallowed grounds are, in a very real way, a kind of tangible fertilizer that empowered the people of what would become Texas to eventually defeat Santa Anna at the Battle of San Jacinto on April 21, 1836. The same could be said of Pearl Harbor. That day of infamy was a turning point that not only called for a response, but demanded it. Reflecting on that day continued to empower the men and women of our armed forces to defeat the enemies that had attacked us. Strange how something tragic, even ominous, can in some way be redeemed.

My wife and I took notice of one of Santa Anna's terrifying methods of executing his prisoners, the "Black Bean." May 14, 1836 marked the day of Texas's independence from Mexico. The Mexican government had forced Santa Anna into retirement because of his great defeat, but it did not last long because disputes with the French caused Santa Anna to emerge from retirement in 1839. A mere two years later, Santa Anna was once again president with dictator power. In October of 1841, Santa Anna ordered Texas prisoners to be marched back to Mexico. Countless prisoners died along the way; a tally of the dead was kept by stringing their ears on a leather thong. San Antonio was invaded by Santa Anna's army in 1842, and in retaliation the Texans seized the town of Mier only to immediately surrender it.

During the march to Mexico, the prisoners revolted and escaped only to be recaptured. As punishment for the attempted escape, Santa Anna decided to execute one man for every ten men that were allowed to live. Each man was blindfolded and forced to draw a bean from a bag. A white bean meant the prisoner went back to the jail. However, if he drew a black bean, the prisoner was executed by firing squad.

A black bean is on display at the Alamo with an appropriate write-up and a letter that one young man wrote to his mother after he had drawn one. It was daunting indeed to read the young fellow's words of dread, of knowing his death was only moments away. He wrote that he hoped that his death would bring meaning to his life.

We are days away from contemplating the day Jesus drew a black bean—a vivid reminder that someday each one of us will draw ours as well. We need to make this a connection, as the passage from Hebrews lays out.

Now how can we, in the same way survivors of the Alamo or

Pearl Harbor did, turn this black bean reminder into something that defeats the darkness? We have to spend some time thinking about death. If we know it is coming, then what are we doing with our lives? What are we allowing Jesus Christ to do in us to help us prepare for that moment? How are we living? How are we preparing to die? Are we prepared for what comes after death? These are the crucial questions we must ask.

I would have hated to have been one of those prisoners who reached in Santa Anna's bean bag, but, in a way, I already have. We have all drawn the black bean; there is no getting around that. Are we prepared for what comes with that? Better yet, are we allowing God to help us prepare for what lies ahead?

— *Another Step . . .* —

Knowing that you have drawn the black bean, what are you doing to prepare for that moment? And for what follows?

A Prayer

God is eternal light.

May I die at peace with my God.

Lord, stay by our door.

—An Early Christian inscription[76]

76 Adalbert-G. Hamman, comp. *Early Christian Prayers* (Chicago: H. Regnery Co., 1961).

Doubt-Proof

Now faith is the assurance of things hoped for, the conviction of things not seen. Indeed, by faith our ancestors received approval. By faith we understand that the worlds were prepared by the word of God, so that what is seen was made from things that are not visible.

—Hebrews 11:1–3

"Do you think people ever doubt that God exists?" was the question one of my pre-adolescent children asked as we stood in line outside of a barbeque joint near the parish I served on the Gulf Coast of Florida. When the question popped out, I was thinking about something that was weighing me down. Standing next to me was one of the little children that Jesus was so fond of, who was thinking on even weightier matters than I.[77] Their good, honest question helped me get out of my mood.

Of course the answer is "Yes."

In the years since, I have had that question put to me more by grown-ups than the youngsters. I think the underlying question is often, "Is it okay to doubt the existence of God?" My answer is only slightly squishy: "It may not be okay, but it is quite normal." I have come to realize the question usually means the one asking is not running away from God, but toward him; they are searching. They have opened their minds and hearts to begin exploring faith.

Peter is probably my favorite of the apostles. The poor and

---

77 Matthew 19:14; Mark 10:14; Luke 18:16.

wonderful man had it right and wrong more than all the others combined. One minute he was confessing Christ, the next minute he was confused about Christ. One minute he was walking on water, and the next he was sinking. One minute pledging his loyalty to Christ, and the next he was denying they had ever met.[78] Of all things mystifying, it was upon this shaky person—whom Jesus nicknamed "The Rock"—that Jesus chose to build the church.[79]

We are told that by the time Jesus's body was growing cold in the tomb, virtually all of the apostles had given up hope. They had three of the best years of seminary education anyone could hope for. They had actually been with Jesus, seen the miracles, heard the words, and felt His touch. Yet by the time the nails were being pulled from the dead flesh, doubt had consumed them and they had run away. Their story reminds me of a line that has been of help to me over the years from Mary Shelley's *Frankenstein*: "Without doubt there would be no need for faith."

Faith gets us through the doubts. Doubts are normal. Alongside the apostles, we are in good company. And we do well to remember Jesus's gentle, loving, and firm reprimand to the most famous doubter, Thomas: "Stop doubting and believe."[80]

The verse from Hebrews is drawn from what is known as the "Great Faith Chapter" of the Bible because it retells the incredible, miraculous stories of God working with his followers over the centuries and how faith played a key role in each case. But faith, like all good things from God, is a gift. It cannot be bought or earned, only received. Many things can block our faith: our reason, intellect, reluctance to be seen as one foolish enough to embrace things that cannot be proven, fear of placing trust in something that may ultimately not be true, and yes, even our doubt. If we can empty ourselves of all those various things that clog our spiritual arteries,

---

78 Matthew 16:13–28; 14:22-35; John 13 and 18.
79 Matthew 16:18.
80 John 20:27.

faith will find its way into our spiritual circulation. What we once doubted, we can embrace as truth.

In the last few days of this daily reader, we will be looking at the primary foci of the entire Christian gospel. Much of what we are told cannot really be proven in a way that we might prove where the first President lived, but we are ultimately not called to live by proof. As the Bible remind us, "The righteous live by faith."[81]

Do people ever doubt the existence of God? Yes, of course. I have. Doubt is normal; it is something with which we all struggle, but ultimately, we are called to a place of faith. How, then, do we find such faith? Know that God wishes to give it. It is a gift. Pray for it. Make sure the stuff that gets in the way of faith is tossed aside. Give yourself the gift of believing in all those wonderful truths shared in God's story.

Christian apologist Josh McDowell puts it this way:

> The most telling testimony of all must be the lives of those early Christians. We must ask ourselves: What caused them to go everywhere telling the message of the risen Christ?
>
> Had there been any visible benefits accruing to them from their efforts—prestige, wealth, increased social status or material benefits—we might logically attempt to account for their actions, for their wholehearted and total allegiance to this "risen Christ."
>
> As a reward for their efforts, however, those early Christians were beaten, stoned to death, thrown to the lions, tortured, crucified. Every conceivable method was used to stop them from talking.
>
> Yes, they were peaceful people. They forced their beliefs on no one. Rather, they laid down their lives as the ultimate proof of their complete confidence in the truth of their message.

---

81 Habakkuk 2:4; Galatians 3:11.

It has been rightly said that they went through the test of death to determine their veracity. It is important to remember that initially the disciples didn't believe. But once convinced—in spite of their doubts—they were never to doubt again that Christ was raised from the dead.[82]

It would be great if there was a pill we could take, an exercise we could do, or a magic mantra we could say that would somehow doubt-proof our journey through the Christian faith. There is not. But there is one thing that might aid us. It springs from a scene in Mark's gospel, and it is as comical as it is profound.

Jesus had just finished saying, "If you are able. All things can be done for the one who believes." Someone immediately jumped up and said, "I believe; help my unbelief."[83] Even the believer needed a little help believing. Maybe that cry, "Help my unbelief," is a good place to start when we are looking for something that is doubt-proof.

— *Another Step . . .* —

What is there in the telling of Christianity that you doubt? Why? And if you did believe, what difference might it make in your life?

---

82 Josh McDowell, *Christianity: Hoax or History?* (Carol Stream: Tyndale House, 1998).
83 Mark 9:23–24.

A Prayer

Give us, O Lord, a steadfast heart, which no unworthy affection may drag downwards; give us an unconquered heart, which no tribulation can wear out; give us an upright heart, which no unworthy purpose may tempt aside. Bestow upon us also, O Lord our God, understanding to know you, diligence to seek you, wisdom to find you and a faithfulness that may finally embrace you; through Jesus Christ our Lord.

—St. Thomas Aquinas, d. 1274[84]

84 Counsell, *2000 Years of Prayer*, 137.

Something New

"I give you a new commandment, that you love one another. Just as I have loved you, you also should love one another. By this everyone will know that you are my disciples, if you have love for one another."

—John 13:34–35

It is kind of hard to wiggle out of Jesus's direct commandment for us to love one another. The Latin phrase used for this poignant moment in the telling of Jesus's last hours on earth is *mandatum novum*, literally translated, new command. It is the story most churches in Christendom tell on Maundy Thursday.

You may think one of the apostles might have piped up and said, "Um, Jesus, don't we have enough commands? I mean really. The Ten Commandments are hard enough, but here You go adding an eleventh." But of course, Jesus's point was to promote the most important commandment. You can obey all of the "Big Ten" and still not love one another. Perhaps the only real way to obey any of the commandments is for our obedience to grow out of love for each other.

Whenever I officiate at a wedding, I take notice that the response of the couple in the liturgy that I use is not "I do," but "I will." What is the difference? "I do" usually implies "I always will." But is that possible? Many of the couples I marry have broken some part of their vows to love, honor, and cherish before the wedding reception is over.

A realistic hope is not that perfection will exist, but the will to get to that place of perfection is always there. Thus, "I will" is possible; "I do" is not. Why?

What if, in marriage, the relationship depended upon what you did, rather than who you were and what you meant to the other? Would it not mean a lifetime of walking on eggshells? Healthy relationships are not grounded in an unrealistic expectation of perfection, but a love of the other, with the hope that love will bear the fruit of right actions. In short, a wedding does not a marriage make; it is a daily loving commitment in the presence of God that makes the marriage. The fruit of that love will be loving actions toward the other. The same is true of any relationship, and perhaps that is what Jesus was trying to knock into the heads of those apostles before he began his journey toward the Cross.

Christianity begins with relationship. God loves us because of who we are, not what we do. God's love is that of a parent toward a child. Our peace, life, and salvation in this life and the life to come is not dependent on our end of the equation. It is found on God's end, God's initiative, God's mercy. Our only appropriate response can be, like grace and faith, to receive.

There is an interesting line in the book of Hebrews that may speak to this tension between how we live, love, and obey all at the same time. The author writes, "For by a single offering he has perfected for all time those who are sanctified" (Hebrews 10:14). This lays out the interesting paradox of the "one sacrifice," which is of course the death of our Lord on the Cross for "the sins of the whole world."[85] It is our embrace of that price paid on our behalf that makes us perfect in God's eyes. Jesus is the lens through which God sees us. But notice, as the Hebrews passage acknowledges, while Jesus "has perfected" (a compound verb that describes a condition—here, perfection), his followers are also being "sanctified" (a compound verb that describes a process—here, sanctification, or the process of being made holy).

Thus, perfect indeed, but at the same time in the process, a kind of ongoing work, of being made holy. We are in this relationship with God not because of what we do, but who we are: the objects of God's love. That love, in return, brings about our obedience.

---

85 John 1:29.

A Christian's morality begins with relationship—an embrace of God's love, which grows within us a love that embraces the other. "By this others will know you are with me," Jesus said, "that you love each other." Perhaps it was another way of saying, "You can obey all the commandments you want, but if you do not love each other, then what difference does obedience make?"

As with marriages, depth often determines strength and breadth. I thank God my wife does not demand my perfection as a price for the love she gives. If she did, I would not make the cut. Thank God, he does not demand my perfection as a price for the love he gives; I would not make that cut either. God's love given should awaken a desire to love in return. With God's help, and with that awakening, we can begin the process toward not only being the husband, wife, friend, or child one should, but the Christian as well.

What Jesus offered on that first Maundy Thursday was something new. Of course, He had been saying it in lots of ways over a number of years in so many places, but the message had not been given that way before, thus the choosing of this night, this moment clearly meant it was, perhaps, the most important farewell address of all.

So, well then, indeed—love one another.

—— *Another Step . . .* ——

How do you experience God's love? How do you share it?

A Prayer

My God, I desire to love thee perfectly, with all
my heart which thou madest for thyself, with all
my mind which only thou canst satisfy, with all
my soul which fain would soar to thee, with all
my strength, my feeble strength, which shrinks
before so great a task, and yet can choose
naught else but spend itself in loving thee.
Claim thou my heart, fill thou my mind, uplift
my soul, and reinforce my strength, that where
I fail thou mayest succeed in me, and make me
love thee perfectly.

—Father Walter Howard Frere, d. 1938[86]

---

86 Counsell, *2000 Years of Prayer*, 400.

The Two Sides of the Cross

So they took Jesus; and carrying the cross by himself,
he went out to what is called The Place of the Skull,
which in Hebrew is called Golgotha. There they crucified Him . . . .

—John 19:16–18

The Passion narrative that unfolds between Maundy Thursday
until that moment when the stone closes across Jesus's tomb has
spawned reflections aplenty, and even more books that look at the
Cross event from all sides. I have added my thoughts in various
places in this volume.

One way of understanding the Cross of Christ is to embrace the
truth that there are two sides. We almost always, to some degree,
live in some sort of tension between these two sides; they spring
to life a bit more during any season of serious reflection. What are
the two sides? The Good Friday side of the Cross and the Easter
side of the Cross.

Everything that happens before Easter is obviously the Good
Friday side. Here we meet with the broken areas of our lives:
temptations, sins, darkness, or, as a friend of mine likes to say,
the attachments that need to be released. On this side of the
Cross there is judgment and we have to come to terms with that.
Romans 3:23 says quite clearly, "All have sinned and fall short of
the glory of God." All means all, not some, or a few, or even most;
all means all. What put Jesus on that Cross was not an angry mob,
an upset religious establishment, or Roman soldiers doing their
job. It was sin: yours, mine, and ours. As we stand on the Good
Friday side, the feeling is morose. A deep desire to be rid of all this

mess should be bubbling up. Here we come to terms with it all: we confess that darkness, we hand it over, and with the grace of God we repent and start life anew.

The Easter side of the Cross promises forgiveness, redemption, and salvation both here and in the life eternal, thank God. That forgiveness is freely given, as none of us was actually there when Jesus was nailed to the Cross. None of us was there when he made the decision to willingly give himself as a ransom for all people everywhere for all time.[87] That is the Easter message: We do not have to live on the Good Friday side of the Cross. With the help of God's grace, we can step from that darkness into the light of resurrection. A resurrection life creeps out in our lives from time to time, but it is really preparing us for a life eternal.

Dietrich Bonhoeffer, a German Lutheran pastor, was executed at an early age by the Nazis only a day or so before his prison was liberated by the allies. He did more in less than four decades than most could do in four lifetimes. Clearly, he had seen both sides of the Cross. Perhaps that is why he wrote, "Only as someone judged by God can a human being live before God. . . . In the form of the Crucified we recognize and find ourselves. Accepted by God, judged and reconciled in the cross: That is the reality of humankind."[88]

Spend some time with the Cross today, perhaps tomorrow as well. By that, I do not mean spend more time bowing as it passes or crossing yourself, but spend time with the Cross. Allow it to judge you. It tells us where the sickness is and where we need the medicine of Christ. When we get a grip on that, then perhaps we can fully appreciate and receive its Easter side.

---

87 Mark 10:45; 1 Timothy 2:6; Hebrews 9:15.

88 Dietrich Bonhoeffer, *Meditations on the Cross* (Louisville: Westminster John Knox, 1998), 51.

— *Another Step . . .* —

Close your eyes for a few moments and meditate on the image of the Cross of Christ. What thoughts, feelings, words, or prayers come to mind?

A Prayer

Forgive them all, O Lord; our sins of omission and our sins of commission; the sins of our youth and the sins of our riper years; the sins of our souls and the sins of our bodies; our secret and our more open sins; our sins of ignorance and surprise, and our more deliberate and presumptuous sins; the sins we have done to please others; the sins we know and remember, and the sins we have forgotten; the sins we have striven to hide from others and the sins by which we have made others offend; forgive them, O Lord, forgive them all for his sake, who died for our sins and rose for our justification, and now stands at the right hand to make intercession for us, Jesus Christ our Lord. *Amen.*

Jesus, poor, unknown and despised, have mercy on us, and let us not be ashamed to follow you. Jesus, accused, and wrongfully condemned, teach us to bear insults patiently, and let us not seek our own glory. Jesus, crowned with thorns and hailed in derision; buffeted, overwhelmed with injuries, grief and humiliations; Jesus, hanging on the accursed tree, bowing the head, giving up the ghost, have mercy on us, and conform our whole lives to your spirit. *Amen.*

—John Wesley, d. 1791[89]

---

89 Counsell, *2000 Years of Prayer*, 314.

Save Us

But as for me, I will look to the Lord, I will wait for the God of my salvation; my God will hear me.

—Micah 7:7

Micah, like all Old Testament prophets, had one real mission: to try to call God's people back into relationship; to not only see, but to embrace God as the source of all comfort, hope, peace, and salvation; to avert their eyes, minds, and hearts away from competing gods, forces, and powers; and to cause reconciliation between Creator and created.

The culmination of the prophet's work is fulfilled in the life, death, and resurrection of Jesus. But we do not get to Easter Sunday without moving through Good Friday and Holy Saturday. We need to maintain, even as our eyes strain for sunrise on Easter morn, what Lord George Carey calls a "Cross spirituality." Such a spirituality calls on us to embrace that the Christian is already dead and yet alive in Christ. If that is the case, then the Christian must embrace the Cross with full force. In his words:

> I must try to live under the cross daily. I must put my Savior always before me as my example, friend, and guide. I must live a life that pleases him. The problem is that it is hard. A friend once remarked: "We are expected to be living sacrifices, but the problem is we keep crawling off the altar." How right he was! How necessary it is for each one of us to apply the cross to our daily lives—to our giving to one another and to

God. . . . Skin deep Christianity will not endure, but heart Christianity will, because it is marked with a cross.[90]

While there are few references in Holy Scripture, the historic statements of faith of the Apostles Creed of the second century, the Nicene Creed of the fourth century, and the Creed of St. Athanasius of the late fifth or early sixth century all tell us that after His death, Jesus Christ descended into hell.[91] The assumption is that the journey between Good Friday and Easter Sunday, for Jesus, ran right through the depth of all creation, a place of utter abandonment from God's presence that surely Jesus felt descending upon him when he cried out, "My God, my God, why have you forsaken me?"[92]

His descent was certainly part of Jesus's taking our place for our sins. It was his most precious act of love in trying to, like the prophets of old, bring God's people back to God. This Holy Saturday pause in the story is a horrific silence that calls us to utter humility before what Christ has done in our stead.

I wrote earlier about my time of service on the Gulf Coast. It was, in many ways, a wonderful season of my life and ministry among loving and active Christians. Only a short drive from white beaches and crystal-clear waters, hardly a day went by when I was not able to behold the hand of God in the beauty of creation. However, sometimes the beauty could turn wicked, as it did in September 2004.

The waters off of Africa produced one of the largest hurricanes in recorded history, Ivan. The storm grew to the size of Texas and slammed into Pensacola, Florida as a strong Category 3 hurricane. The worst of the storm lasted nearly twelve hours. When it was over, more than 25,000 homes were either destroyed or had sustained major damage. Hundreds of businesses were affected, several people were killed, and many others injured.

---

90 Carey, *I Believe*, 125.
91 Matthew 12:40; Ephesians 4:9–10; 1 Peter 3:19.
92 Matthew 27:46.

For all kinds of reasons, my wife and I decided to ride out the storm in our home with our three children. Sometime in the night, we began to feel we had made a terrible decision. The winds were literally howling. News reports a few days later would tell that dozens of tornadoes skipped down through the area and wreaked havoc. We lived a short walk from Escambia Bay, where the winds forced the water, which had no place to go, into a fifty-foot tidal wave that tore the Interstate Highway 10 bridge in half. Virtually all the homes on the eastern shore of the bay were destroyed. And it was all going on while we were huddled in one room of our house with a small kerosene lamp.

Around 2:00 a.m. the winds reached their worst. We could hear the crash of trees and limbs falling on every side of the house. The plywood we had used to cover our windows was either beginning to blow off or flap like a playing card. It was then that my wife got out one of our family prayer books and turned to a service that had often brought us comfort in times of incredible distress, Compline.

"The Lord Almighty grant us a peaceful night and a perfect end. Amen," we prayed together. Would it be the end? We did not know. We prayed the confession of sin and then the words we repeated again and again until dawn's early light, "O God, make speed to save us. O Lord, make haste to help us."[93]

Nothing else gave us peace on that night—not money, health, even our home. We finally had to put all that we were and would be in God's hands. When dawn came, we emerged from our home. It looked like a giant had walked in a circle around our house; fallen trees literally encircled it.

I am not one who believes God saves this house or that person because he plays favorites. It did not matter how we got through the night, nor did it really matter what went on outside our doors. What mattered was that the only real eye of the storm was holding fast to one another and to God. It was a long, long night, but dawn came again and we were safe and saved.

---

93 Book of Common Prayer, 128.

The journey between Good Friday and Easter Sunday was a long, long night. In that season of spiritual pregnancy, one can do nothing but wait for what rests with the first sunrise of a world that would soon know Resurrection. And holding on to that alone will not only make us safe, but will also save us.

— *Another Step . . .* —

Think on a "Holy Saturday" in your life. How did you wait that season out? Where did you encounter the peace of God?

A Prayer

Our darkness is never darkness in your sight;
The deepest night is clear as the daylight.
Stay with me, remain here with me,
Watch and pray, watch and pray.
Wait for the Lord, whose day is near.
Wait for the Lord: keep watch, take heart!
Within our darkest night, you kindle the fire
That never dies away, that never dies away.

—A prayer of the Taizé Community

The Way . . . Out

The women were terrified and bowed their faces to the ground, but the men said to them, "Why do you look for the living among the dead? He is not here, but has risen."

—Luke 24:5

One of my closest friends and most trusted advisors is a recovering alcoholic and former cocaine and gambling addict. He used to tell me that for many of his young adult years, he was in the grip of this "triple threat." Through the help of friends, a community of faith and trust in God, he escaped their clutches, recovered, and went on to live a life that no one, not even he, could have imagined when he was in his darkest moments. In my pastoral work when I encounter someone with similar addictions, while I would pray with them and offer what spiritual comfort I could, often my next step was to put them in touch with my friend because he had been where they were and could help show them the way out.

As we have traveled the journey of this book from the first page, we have been reflecting on several views of the Christian story through the prism of a God who wants to be in a relationship with us so much so that he finally came in human form. To quote Lord Carey once more, "Here is a Messiah who by becoming one of us knows all about human weakness, about human life and development. He knows all about sadness, temptation and the grubby facts of life. I can take comfort in this, knowing that my Lord has entered into our humanity and brought it home to God."[94]

---

94 Carey, *I Believe*, 104.

It was this same Messiah who was able to survive betrayal, torture, execution, even hell itself. When it was all over, Jesus stepped from the grave to show that God's power was, and is, greater than any darkness of which we humans can dream. That is why, when all is said and done, it is so important that we who bear the name Christian turn to Christ. He has been where we will go and can help show us the way out.

We began this journey with that stark reminder, "Remember you are dust, and to dust you shall return." Those words are supposed to remind us of our deaths and the sin that causes them. Death was not God's original plan; we started all of that by turning from God to self. Once that happened, there was no turning back—sin infected humanity and still does today.

Thankfully, God loved us so much that he could not just leave us in our sin and death, but sent Christ into the world to save sinners like you and me.[95] Love compelled God to share creation with us, and love compelled God to come—in the person of Christ to live among us—so that new life might be restored where it had been corrupted. As my mentor John Claypool used to say to me, "Remember, the last things are not the worst things." How to face those last things? Turn to Christ and, lo and behold, we encounter the expert not just in survival, but resurrection. Take his hand and hear his words, "Peace be with you," as he steps from the grave, and we will come to know not just the possibility, but the reality of Resurrection.

When I was young, one of my favorite movies was Audie Murphy's *To Hell and Back*, which told the actor's own incredible story of defeating an army of Nazi soldiers virtually on his own. A few years back I visited his grave at Arlington National Cemetery, and I remember goosebumps appearing on my arms as I stood close to the remains of a man who had faced death up close and personal and yet had survived.

Our story says that Jesus really did go to hell and back, but his remains are nowhere to be found because for Jesus, death was not

---

95 1 Timothy 1:15.

the last word. Jesus responded to our betrayal with forgiveness, to our torture with endurance, to our execution with submission, to death with commendation, and to hell with embrace. But when it was all over, Jesus pronounced victory over each. He has been there, lived through it all, and finally conquered it all.

I suppose some people might question my trust in a friend who had lived in so many dark places. I did not because I knew him and also knew him to be trustworthy. I felt it was worth the risk. And I suppose some people might question my giving my life and life's work to one who claimed to make it to hell and back. But I do not, because I have come to know him as best as my faculties and faith will allow, and I have found him to be trustworthy. And I feel it is worth the risk.

But then is it a risk? Not really. I love the scene from Luke's gospel when the women find the tomb empty. At first they are terrified, but the angel says, "Why do you look for the living among the dead? He is not here, He is risen." Wow! Those are good words for any who face darkness in their lives. And they are even better words for all of us who might find the idea of death just a bit daunting, if not terrifying, because Christ has been where we will go and if we turn to him, he will show us the way out.

—   *Another Step . . .*   —

What does the promise of Easter mean for the empty tombs of your life? And what does it mean for you as we all face the door of death?

A Prayer

Most Glorious Lord of Life! That, on this day,
Didst make thy triumph over death and sin;
And, having harrowed hell, didst bring away
Captivity thence captive, us to win:
This joyous day, dear Lord, with joy begin;
And grant that we, for whom thou didst die,
Being with thy dear blood clean washed from sin,
May live forever in felicity!
And that thy love we weighing worthily,
May likewise love thee for the same again;
And for thy sake, that all like dear didst buy,
With love may one another entertain!
So let us love, dear Love, like as we ought,
Love is the lesson which the Lord us taught.

—Edmund Spenser, d. 1599[96]

---

96 Counsell, *2000 Years of Prayer*, 226–227.

Afterword

Well?

> Now when Jesus came into the district of Caesarea
> Philippi, he asked his disciples, "Who do people say
> that the Son of Man is?" And they said, "Some say John
> the Baptist, but others Elijah, and still others Jeremiah
> or one of the prophets." He said to them, "But who do
> you say that I am?" Simon Peter answered, "You are
> the Messiah, the Son of the living God." And Jesus
> answered him, "Blessed are you, Simon son of Jonah!
> For flesh and blood has not revealed this to you, but my
> Father in heaven." — Matthew 16:13–17

In a few of the meditations I have offered, I have concluded
with the word, "Well?" I confess that I picked that up from my
mentor, John Claypool. John often ended his sermon with that
probing word, hoping that someone out there hearing him might
take his words past the ears and head and into heart and soul.

Let me fess up. The underlying agenda of this work is not only
to offer scripture passages, various insights, provoking thoughts,
and prayers about a life in Christ Jesus but also to provide you
an opportunity to step more deeply into that life, and perhaps for
some, for the very first time.

The confession of Peter, which we read about in Matthew's
gospel above, was a key moment in the life and ministry of Jesus.
Caesarea Philippi was actually a rather pagan city with lots of competing philosophies, religions, preachers, and prophets. Perhaps it
was for this reason, this moment, and in this city that Jesus chose
to ask the apostles the most important question of his time. "Who
do people say that I am?"

It was not that he did not know; it was that he wanted to see
if they knew. Did these, the closest twelve who would carry the

message forward, "get it"? At first, clearly most did not. They begin to pitch out answers like junior high school students scrambling to answer the teacher's question when no one has studied the material.

Then Jesus zoomed in on Peter: "But what about you, who do you say that I am?"

Peter took a deep breath and named it, hitting the proverbial nail on the head, "You are the Messiah, the Son of the living God."

And Jesus said, "Blessed are you Simon!" In other words, "By George, you've got it!" Jesus went on to tell Peter and the other apostles that it is upon Peter and this confession that Jesus would build the church.

The goal of my writing is to remind you, me, and anyone who reads it that as Christians we are called to give our lives to Jesus Christ. Another of my mentors, the late Anglican theologian and pastor John Stott put it this way:

> A Christian is somebody personally related to Jesus Christ. Christianity without Christ is a chest without a treasure, a frame without a portrait, a corpse without breath. Christ comes to each of us with an individual summons: "Come to me," "follow me." And the Christian life begins as, however hesitantly and falteringly, we respond to his call. Then as we start following him, we discover to our increasing and delighted surprise, that a personal relationship to Christ is a many-sided, many-colored, many-splendored thing. We find that he is our mediator and our foundation, our life-giver and our lord, the secret and the goal of our living, our lover and our model... We learn that to be a Christian is to live our lives through, on, in, under, with, unto, for and like Jesus Christ. Each preposition indicates a different kind of relationship, but in each case Christ himself is at the centre.[97]

---

97 John Stott, *Life in Christ* (Wheaton, IL; Tyndale House Publishers, Inc., 1991), 111.

As I was preparing this final piece, I realized that it was thirty years ago, almost to the day, when I made the "hesitant and faltering" response of which Stott writes. Thanks to the consistent pressing of my father and mother, church was always part of my life. I was baptized as an infant, grew up in Sunday school, learned the hymns, and went to Vacation Bible School and youth group. As a teen, I was confirmed into the church. God was clearly at work in and through all those moments.

God comes to us in many ways. The diversity of God's children means we come to God in different ways. Since I was a child, God had been part of my life, but had I actually decided to follow Him? The answer was no. I began to encounter many people, young and old, who spoke of a relationship with Christ. They described it in all kinds of ways: born again, renewal, commitment, conversion, coming to Christ. For some, it was a specific moment, like a church service or crusade; for others it was a lifetime journey, something that they had simply always known. Some really did make this decision at their Confirmation or Baptism; others—like me—did not. Whatever "it" was, I knew I wanted it. I wanted that personal relationship with Christ.

I spent a great deal of time with various clergy those three decades ago. One afternoon, I was sitting by a friend's pool with a campus minister asking all kinds of questions. Finally, with a smile, he said, "You know, we can sit and ask and answer questions all afternoon, but I think what you are really looking for is a relationship with Christ. Have you made the decision to follow him?"

I was honest enough to say, "You know, I am not sure." The minister smiled and said, "Why don't you think about that and then we can get to the questions." It was a good provoking thought. I spent the rest of the day reflecting on the many times I had conversations in the previous months with people about this relationship I desired. I also spent a great deal of time pondering my religious history. Baptism, check. Confirmation, check. Sunday school, check. Bible reader, check. Nightly prayers, check. Decision to follow, to really give my life to Christ? No check.

That night after supper, I went up to my room, closed my door, got down on my knees, and prayed. I cannot tell you what I prayed or how I prayed it. I only know that I offered my life to Christ to be a follower, to be a disciple. I wanted not just to say I was a Christian, I wanted to be a Christian.

I remember finishing the prayer with some hope that an angel would appear, music would swell, light would fill the room. Nothing. I got up off my knees and went to bed without any spiritual earthquake whatsoever. The next morning as I opened my eyes I noticed one thing: the presence of God. Not a physical presence, just a kind of reality that Jesus was not a historical figure, but was now part of who I was, and I part of him; I had been grafted into him. There has never been a day in my life since that moment that I have not known the presence of Christ in my life.

I was not perfect at that moment nor am I now. There were many things I did, and perhaps have done today, after that moment that did not look at all Christ-like. There have been days when I have been terribly mad or upset with Christ; others when I have doubted him and his work in my life and the world. There have been days when he has, by my sinful human interpretation, disappointed me, and many more that I have disappointed him. There have been days when Jesus has shown up where I never expected and days when I thought He would be there, but he never came as I wanted. There have been days when he has felt as far away as the next galaxy and others when he is as close as the bread and wine at communion. The point is that the relationship began and He has always, always been faithful even when I am not.

I wonder if you have made that decision? Sometimes we need to "re-make it." And really the point is not how you do it, but if you do it. You do not have to be in any kind of particular place or state of being. Sometimes it is in a moment of terror or after a spiritual encounter, sometimes when you have been really forgiven or moved by injustice in the world, maybe in a religious service or in the privacy of your bedroom. I think the point is just to invite Him in and let Him get to work.

In 1961, Irving Stone wrote a biographical novel, *The Agony and the Ecstasy*, about the life of sculptor Michelangelo Buonarroti. A few years later, a portion of the novel that focused on the painting of the Sistine Chapel was made into a major film of the same name, starring Charlton Heston as Michelangelo and Rex Harrison as Pope Julius II. If you know the film, you know there is a great deal of conflict, initially, between Michelangelo and the pope. They haggled over price and design, how long it would take and what the final product would look like. Finally, they agreed and the artist moved into place. He sets up his scaffolding and gets to work. Almost from the beginning, Pope Julius, anxious to have a complete product came into the chapel and yelled up at the artist, "When will you make an end of it?"

Michelangelo looks down, usually with some instrument hanging from his hand or brush from his lips and answered, "When I am finished!"

What was he doing? Why was it taking so long? He was patching the holes, filling in the cracks, sanding the rough spots, so he could draw the design, fill it in slowly and deliberately, until it was just right. But every few weeks, in popped the Pope, "When will you make an end of it?"

"When I am finished!"

As the movie reaches its end, we find both the pope and the artist late in life, both struggling with health issues, both having given so much of themselves to this project. The pope thought he would not live to see it, but then he rallies. Julius approaches the chapel and large, heavy curtains are pulled back. Music swells; no words are spoken—the director, Carol Reid, offers the simple and profound gift of the vision of the beauty created once the artist has been able to move into the chapel and complete his work.

At times, we can be like Pope Julius. We want to be perfect or whole, we want all our questions answered and our doubts wiped away, but it does not work that way. What God says to us in Christ is, "Just let me move in, let me set up shop; if you trust me I will get to work. I will patch up the holes, fill in the cracks, sand down the rough spots making you the creature you have always wanted to be. You may get impatient and you may ask me to finish, but trust me. If you invite me in, I am in to stay and I am working, creating a beautiful chapel in you that you may not even see until you slip from this life to the next. But when you do and the curtain is pulled back, what you will find will be a vision you cannot even comprehend."

I have ended each meditation with a closing thought that I have called "Another Step." The title of this book, *A Path to Wholeness* was chosen purposely. This book is offered as a gift—it is a collection of words, thoughts and reflections that offer "a" path, not the "only" path—just "a path." But the intent remains: a tool, a stepping-stone perhaps that hopefully will take you toward that place for which every soul hungers—life, peace, shalom—wholeness.

I have also included in each meditation a prayer from either our Christian tradition or in some cases a prayer I have written. But I will not close that way. I invite you to come up with "Another Step" of your own, and a prayer to respond to it. If you already know and serve our Lord, I pray this book has fed you in some way. If you have a need to step more deeply, then I pray you will do that as well. And if you have yet to invite that great artist within the chapel of your heart, I encourage you to do that today, in your own prayer with your own words.

Well? Amen.

Acknowledgments

There is a wonderful tradition among our Jewish forbears of offering grace "after" meals. The offering of a special benediction, in Hebrew, *birkat ha-mazon*, came in response to the biblical injunction from Deuteronomy 8:10, "And you shall eat and be satisfied, and bless the Lord your God."

We have come now to the end of *A Path to Wholeness*, and while I was certainly grateful to be invited by Church Publishing to offer you this book, now that it has come to a close, I offer a word of thanks to all who made this possible.

Foremost in my list of thanks comes my wife, Laura, who supports my work and is my most honest and most gentle critic, as well as my first and always fierce and unapologetic advocate, defender, and supporter. I am grateful as well to my children and grandchildren, who have supported my writing ministry for many decades now through their encouragement and patience, allowing me to sequester myself for hours, and sometimes days, on end. The parish I now serve, St. Martin's Episcopal Church in Houston has been very generous in supporting this venue of ministry, and I continue to count it a tremendous blessing to serve her people as their rector, priest, pastor, and friend. They are, indeed, a wider circle of family.

A word of thanks for sure to the first readers of this manuscript, who encouraged me to step beyond my private study and share the words more widely: the Rev. Dr. Fisher Humprheys, my doctoral advisor and first publisher; the Most Right Honorable George L. Carey, 103rd archbishop of Canterbury, who has been a wonderful mentor and dear friend for nearly two decades; and the Very Rev. Ian Markham, dean and president of Virginia Theological Seminary.

And now to my many new friends with Church Publishing. This is my fourth book with Church Publishing, the others being

Bits of Heaven, Finding Shelter, and *Preparing Room*; and my sixth project overall, having contributed by writing a forward to the newly revised *Tracks of a Fellow Struggler,* by my mentor and father in the faith, the late Rev. Dr. John Claypool, and as a contributor to *Prophetic Preaching: The Hope or the Curse of the Church?,* edited by Ian Markham. From beginning to end of each project I never felt as if I was part of a publishing machine, churning out work for the mere purpose of adding more volumes to someone's shelves. Instead, I have felt part of a circle of encouraging family members—cheering me on, being patient with me, tenderly and kindly offering suggestions and edits that made my words more clear, cogent, and readable. So, among those, I offer my thanks to my publisher, Nancy Bryan; my careful editor, Milton Brasher-Cunningham; Ryan Masteller, the production manager, who organizes and orders everyone's work so that the end product is what you now hold in your hands.

And frankly, whatever I have shared with Church Publishing has almost always passed through the very capable hands of my colleagues; Aleeta Bureau, David Bolin, and Sue Davis in the communications department of St. Martin's; and my friends and the comrades with whom I work in the rector's office; my executive assistant, Lesley Hough; my administrative associate, Carol Gallion; and my administrative assistants, Brittney Pena and Allie Hippard. These fine folk not only help me keep things in order, they also help me jealously guard my calendar so I can carry out my duties as rector of St. Martin's, as well as this writing ministry to which I also feel called.

I would be remiss if I did not also thank you, my patient reader. One never knows if his or her written words have an impact on the lives of others. As I began this work, that was, and continues to be, my hope; and if you have read cover to cover and now come upon these last words, that hope remains. It is my prayer that these words have perhaps helped in some way—encouraged growth, aided in transformation, shifted your internal tectonic plates in some way that you feel closer to being whole than you were when you first picked up this little book.

Then lastly, and most importantly, I am grateful to God, his Son the Lord of Light and Life, and to the Spirit, Who comforts, converts, convicts, and remains a constant companion on my own path to wholeness. I hope and pray that you will find what I have found on that path—the love and shalom there is in the wide arms of our great Shepherd.

RJL+

Scriptural Index

Index of Authors Cited